EXECUTIVE RETIREMENT

and

EFFECTIVE MANAGEMENT

By
RICHARD A. BEAUMONT
JAMES W. TOWER

Industrial Relations Monograph, No. 20
INDUSTRIAL RELATIONS COUNSELORS, INC.
New York: 1961

Manufactured in the United States of America by
The Haddon Craftsmen, Inc., Scranton, Pa.

INDUSTRIAL RELATIONS COUNSELORS, INC.

Industrial Relations Counselors, Inc., is a nonprofit research and educational organization, founded in 1926. It is dedicated, by its charter, "To advance the knowledge and practice of human relationships in industry, commerce, education and government."

At the time of its formation, Industrial Relations Counselors was the only organization in the country specializing in industrial relations research and its practical application. The research activities of Industrial Relations Counselors have been facilitated over the years by its continued close relations with an ever-growing number of companies representing a cross section of industry and commerce, both here and abroad, and with governmental, professional, educational, and other groups interested in this field of research.

Industrial Relations Counselors has issued numerous studies over the years which analyze and evaluate trends, needs and opportunities, as well as current experience, in the industrial relations field. A list of these studies is available on request.

THE BOARD OF TRUSTEES

The Industrial Relations Counselors research program is conducted with the advice and guidance of a distinguished Board of Trustees, which meets regularly to review plans and progress. The members of this Board are:

FOREWORD

In the United States there has been increasingly widespread concern with the growing number of people in that segment of the population referred to as the aged. This has led to a series of investigations into the personal, social and economic considerations involved in retirement in general, and much research is being carried out to broaden understanding in this area.

Equally important, however, are the problems imposed upon organizations because of the fact that people age and move into retirement. Viewing retirement as an organizational or corporate matter leads to an interesting set of questions. When is the best time to retire a man? How can retirement be related to the achievement of corporate objectives? What is the influence of retirement on the continuing efficiency of older men? All of these questions are significant, but especially when they are directed toward the executive group of an organization.

This study, therefore, focuses on the corporate problems faced in executive retirement. Its purpose is to isolate the practices and problems in executive retirement, in the interests of companies as well as for students of the corporate process. The findings of the study show that executive retirement is a matter of central importance to management, and it is far more complicated than simply deciding when to retire a man. Executive retirement is tied to over-all staffing; effective policies and practices in this area can therefore help a company maximize its utilization of its executive staff.

This study, by Richard A. Beaumont and James W. Tower of the Industrial Relations Counselors staff, is based on a survey conducted during the twelve-month period beginning September, 1959. Appreciation of a magnitude not to be encompassed in a foreword is here expressed briefly on behalf of IRC and the authors to two groups. First, the study could not have been undertaken without the financial support given to it by Mr. Rodman Rockefeller, the Alfred P. Sloan Foundation, the Rockefeller Brothers Fund and the Ford Foundation. It is equally true that the study would not have been possible without the co-operation of the hundreds of executives who gave generously of their time and experience in interviews, who filled out questionnaires, and otherwise contributed to the substance of the work. By original commitment, they and their companies shall remain anonymous.

The authors express appreciation to other members of the staff for their interest and comments in the several stages of the study, but especially for the constructive assistance given by their colleague, Maud B. Patten, and to Sheila R. Hough for analyzing and classifying the mass of data received. Appreciation also is extended to James H. Taylor, chairman of the IRC Advisory Board for Research, whose review of the manuscript and comments were of great value to the authors.

CARROLL E. FRENCH, *President*
Industrial Relations Counselors, Inc.

New York City, February 15, 1961

CONTENTS

vii

Executive Retirement
and
Effective Management

CHAPTER I

Introduction

INTERRELATING PEOPLE with the objectives of the enterprise to the advantage of both is one of the major problems of a modern industrialized society. It is this problem that gives rise to all aspects of personnel and human relations, and which attracts the attention of practitioners and scholars who study case situations in an attempt to develop general theories about human behavior, work and output. Such studies usually seek out situations where a breakdown or conflict has occurred in relationships between an enterprise and its people. The issues connected with retirement of people do not, however, generate breakdowns or conflicts, yet significant situations have to be dealt with constantly as people age and approach retirement.

Problems of older people are being more aggressively studied now than ever before. Generally, such studies have taken the broad social and economic approaches, or have been concerned only with the reactions of individuals to anticipated retirement or the fact of retirement, in terms of personal adjustment. The broader studies indicate a development of far-reaching problems for the nation, unless it is possible to view the matter of retirement in new and different ways. Implicit in many such studies is the importance of retirement practices in companies as they affect individuals, yet very little attention has been given to the problems and concerns of companies which arise from the aging of employees. But these corporate problems must be considered, for corporate retirement practices are directly related to the achievement of more efficient and productive operations. In turn, productive operations provide the means for the nation to support an ever increasing older population. Applying a retirement policy to the executive group in a company is especially crucial, for the destiny of corporations, and indeed the corporate system itself, depends on the abilities and actions of those at the executive level. A study of executive retirement as a company problem is therefore timely.

A. NATURE OF THE RETIREMENT PROBLEM

The problem of retirement is a multidimensional one. It is a broad *social* problem, in that it affects the roles and status of people and may remove valued skills and accumulated knowledge from society. . . . It is an important *economic* issue, in that it affects the utilization of manpower and, from the national economic point of view, retiring people who could still make a contribution through work may mean that others must assist in supporting them. . . . It is a *management* problem, for needed continuity of viewpoint, skills and vigor in an organization may be affected when, through application of a mandatory retirement age, important talents are withdrawn from an enterprise, or, conversely, when older employees who are no longer able to perform their jobs fully are retained. . . . It is an *individual* problem, for the retiree and his family may not be prepared for retirement—financially, emotionally, or otherwise. . . . It is a problem to *younger people,* because, if older persons are not retired on a regular basis, the younger ones may feel that they are restricted in their personal development and advancement within an organization.

The retirement problem in all its dimensions is but another challenge to the private enterprise system. Over the years corporations have evidenced their ability to be fluid and to change in response to public demands and constantly shifting needs of the economy, so that, today the corporate system is woven into the fabric of our political and economic life. This idea has been expressed as follows: "The industrial revolution, as it spread over twentieth-century life, required collective organization of men and things. To bring its human structure and physical plant into existence, to carry out its operations, to distribute its products, to meet the growing demands made on it in peace and war, proved wholly beyond the capacity of individual entrepreneurs. As the twentieth century moves into afternoon, two systems—and (thus far) two only—have emerged as vehicles of modern industrial economics. One is the socialist commissariat; its highest organization at present is in the Soviet Union. The other is the modern corporation, most highly developed in the United States."[1]

[1] Foreword by A. A. Berle, Jr., in *The Corporation in Modern Society,* Edward S. Mason, ed., Cambridge: Harvard University Press, 1959, p. ix.

1. The Corporate Problem

It is easy to be dazzled into thinking that our modern corporations are invulnerable, with their integrated plants and plant facilities, their fantastic output potential, and their strength and endurance. But the success of the corporate system is determined in large part through the continuity it provides in the development, production and distribution of goods and services of economic value. This continuity is achieved through the perpetual life of the corporation and a succession of increasingly capable managers. Sometimes elaborate systems are devised, as this study shows, to insure a smooth transfer of responsibility and to minimize the loss to a company of those who have made a marked contribution to its success.

A study of corporate problems and practices in executive retirement is to some extent a study of the maturation process of a company. It is also a study of a company's responses to the peculiar pressures imposed on it in the financial and product markets in which it moves. An inventive genius has an impact on a young company that is immeasurable. A Steinmetz in his day, or the "egghead" millionaires in their electronic firms today,[2] are cases in point. At other stages of a corporation's development an administrative, organizational, financial, marketing or production genius may be needed to enable a company to achieve growth. But at some point in the evolutionary development of the corporation it is improbable that any single individual can affect the organization so deeply or in the same way as when the enterprise was younger or smaller. Retirement practices seem to reflect these differences in corporate maturity.

The nature of the corporate problem arising from the aging of men is obvious, and can be viewed from four per-

[2] See the discussion in *Fortune*, September, 1960, p. 172.

spectives. The first is in terms of the effects of aging. At some point a man must be retired because he is no longer able to, or no longer wishes to, contribute to the company to the degree that the company needs and desires. This may be a matter of his motivation, his inability to adjust to new situations, or the actual breakdown of his mental or physical capabilities.

Secondly, there may be a problem at the other end of the employment system, with younger men. One can conceive of younger executives becoming restive as they wait for older men to move up, or into retirement, thereby opening up choice places in the executive hierarchy. Thus, as a matter of retaining younger competent men on whom the future of the corporation rests, it may be necessary to insure the separation of older executives through forced retirement.

The third perspective from which the executive retirement problem may be viewed is in terms of the mechanical administration of the promotional and retirement system within a company. Handling retirement as a regularized and predictable process permits an organization to plan for the retirement of an executive and for replacements that will be needed at a certain time in the future. A formal retirement system with a fixed retirement age is, therefore, a far more comprehensible method of assuring transition, some hold, than if a company has to respond to the uncertainty of varied patterns of aging among executives.

Finally, and closely related to the administrative issues in retirement, is viewing executive retirement decisions as a problem among peers. A normal or mandatory age provides a standard for determining when a colleague or boss is to retire. Thus, executives do not become involved in what might be an onerous or distasteful decision to make.

Considering the corporate problem in these terms is more meaningful than to confine the discussion to the traditional arguments over "fixed retirement" versus "flexible retirement." This study is not designed to support fixed or flexible retirement approaches, but rather to examine the reasons for the one or the other, and the actual conditions that seem to support a company's approach one way or the other.

2. The Executive's Problem

Although this study is directed toward corporate problems and practices in executive retirement, some comments must be made on the attitudes of executives toward the prospect and the fact of being retired. These attitudes necessarily reflect attitudes toward work, but also toward life as a whole. Many executives see the job as the central fact of life, for it gives a sense of purpose, or has in part adapted a man's inherent sense of personal purpose to the demands of the business. It gives an executive authority over people and things; it rewards him tangibly and intangibly; it makes demands on him which he meets with good spirit or bad.

Much has been written about what employees seek from their jobs, their employment, their employers; less has been developed about the meaning of work in the lives of individuals in today's society. Conventional polls of attitudes among representative groups of lower echelon employees disclose that security and compatibility rank along with money as motivations,[3] but such analyses do not meld the several factors into a meaningful totality of the values of a job. Determining the meaning of work for the executive is most complicated. Lerner speaks of the executive's position as characterized by "success, prestige, money, power and secu-

[3] Eugene A. Friedmann and Robert J. Havighurst, *The Meaning of Work and Retirement,* Chicago: University of Chicago Press, p. 173.

rity,"[4] but it is noteworthy that at least three of these deteriorate or are eliminated by retirement.

In most instances executives see their work as having a high degree of social usefulness and of service to shareholders, subordinates, customers. At the executive level, there is often a real sense of having fiduciary responsibility for the corporation. But beyond the commercial aspects of profits and growth, sales curves and cost reduction, many people see the corporation as the instrument which makes the economic system work. Thus, in a sense each executive is contributing to and is a custodian of the welfare of the nation. To the extent that an executive holds this view of his role, he may find retirement the more difficult.

Executive responsibility is accompanied by a vested authority to direct and control. Authority may encompass part or all of a business which may be a powerful instrument in the total economy. Authority implies not only responsibility for the conservation and growth of others' investments in the firm, but also freedom (and maybe the obligation) to experiment, to expand, to anticipate external competition and trends. The executive can issue orders. The authority affecting people finds constructive outlet in giving subordinates opportunities to grow to self-fulfillment, but always with prime regard to the corporate interests, and this is a major source of satisfaction claimed by many executives.

Retirement from active executive office means, typically, complete loss of the authority of such office. The retired executive has no subordinates to advise, control, develop, and inspire. His span of control is suddenly limited to his family . . . and the man who mows the lawn. The substance

[4] Max Lerner, *America As A Civilization*, New York: Simon and Schuster, p. 689.

of the specialized knowledge, judgment and decisiveness which have typified his actions for decades is nullified.

The meanings for the executive of monetary rewards are obvious, but the real satisfactions derived from the typical pattern of executive compensation may not be the relatively high level of income, but the ever present possibility of making more money. For executive action is a gamble, in the sense that never is it a sure thing that the new product line, or the new appointment, or the new plans for financing will work out as planned, and there is fun in it.

Aside from the evidences of authority, and the tangible aspects of compensation and personal security in work, is the factor of prestige. There is a sense of self-fulfillment in a ranking executive title, especially in association with a successful enterprise. Friendships and social relationships arise from and supplement the relationships at the office. By middle age, many executives have few friends with whom there is no business relationship. Practically all the evidence and symbols of prestige inherent in executive office vanish on retirement; the friendships with colleagues are undermined, because the retired executive is no longer a party to the daily work.

Among the broad areas of significance and meaning attributed to work is the precedence given by the executive to job demands over other demands. The job comes first. Long-expected vacations are abandoned because of crises "at the office." Executives work long hours, taking home the reports to be read and the reports to be written. Social activities seem almost to be sessions adjourned from the conference room, and there is usually a direct or indirect business purpose to the list of invitations for dinner, for golf, or for hunting. There are executives who work for their companies only between nine and five, and take their vacations as scheduled; but many speak with pride of their subordination of everything else to what they see as the demands of the corporation.

Like other humans, executives tend to be creatures of habit and routine, and the sharp break in the routine of existence implicit in retirement may be one of the most serious significances of the issue. The pressures of decisions and crises are replaced by the vacuum of no decisions to make; the demands of time are no longer of great consequence; self-denial is displaced by self-indulgence, in violation of the nominally spartan code of self-abnegation which some executives impose on themselves. Retirement, whether a distant eventuality for the youthful executive, or a more immediate prospect for the executive in his mid-fifties, or a definite date and quite imminent for the man in his sixties, demands facing up to the whole continuum of successes and triumphs, of promotion and nonpromotion, to the question of the value of what the individual has accomplished and how he may adjust to and make useful the days remaining to him.

B. METHOD OF SURVEYING THE PROBLEM

Corporate practices and problems in executive retirement are a most sensitive indicator of the balance between corporate and personal goals and objectives. Considering retirement among executives in terms of the interests and objectives of companies is obviously only part of the total problem of the aging. But for the corporation it is the significant one. It involves the retaining of valuable skills or knowledge, making effective transitions from a retiring executive to his replacement, administering a program of retirement that is sensible for the organization, and maintaining incentives for both younger and older executives—

all based on the pattern of executive retirement within a company.

Coverage of the study was limited to retirement practices affecting only the executive group in a company, and there are several reasons for devoting attention to that group in particular:

1. Executives may not be affected by age in the same way as employees who perform manual or routine duties, and thus they may continue to make unique contributions to the company despite their age.

2. Executives are generally in far greater demand than other employees, and the shortage of executive talent continues, which means that companies may have to continue to find executive skills among older workers.

3. Where formal policies exist, a company is more likely to modify its policy for the executive group than for other groups in the company, because of the nature of the contribution which an executive may be in a position to make on behalf of the company or in his relationship to other policy makers.

4. It is with the executive group that possible shortcomings of retirement policy come clearly into focus, as a company struggles to resolve the difficulties that arise when the aging process takes a toll among executives.

5. The executive is likely to be far more dedicated to his work and, therefore, devotes less attention to outside interests than other employees. Hence, retirement is likely to have a greater impact on the executive personally, and thus would be expected to arouse a greater reaction to corporate retirement policies—particularly when the aging executive himself is involved in developing the organization's retirement policy.

6. An executive may not only be an official of the company but may have an ownership interest in it, and this factor might influence the shaping of retirement policy.

The significance of such factors as these, in terms of how they create corporate problems and influence practices in retirement, could be determined only by observing the strains, modifications and possible changes imposed on company policy because of the role of men in the key executive group.

1. Defining the Executive Group

Crucial to the study was the defining of "executive," to insure that a relatively homogeneous group of positions was being considered in the various types of company situations in the survey group. Defining the term "executive" is a particularly difficult and elusive task. It is interesting to note that difficulty with definition is not unusual. Economists have struggled with it over the years. To Adam Smith, the executive was the entrepreneur and the holder of capital. While Smith did not have great trouble with definition, later economists did, because of the increased separation between owner and manager.

It was John Maynard Keynes who finally put his finger on the core of the executive function when he spoke of the man who is the mainspring of the productive process. The executive or manager is the man who makes the decisions that turn the productive process on or off. This is the man who determines the corporation's thrust in the market place and its ability to survive market competition. And it is this man who was looked for in this study, for such men make identifiable contributions to the corporation, thereby making it most difficult to adjust to the fact of their retirement.

The detailed definition of who would be considered an executive for purposes of this study is shown in Appendix A. In condensed form, it identifies the executive groups in companies as follows:

They are the highest paid group in the company, generally constituting the highest four levels of management responsibility on a corporate organization chart. Included are those who, regardless of title, are the managers, specialists, or staff advisers who direct, or influence the direction of, the various functional areas of a company, at the headquarters, divisional and plant levels.

Obviously, company size, organization structure and individual responsibility contribute to the determination of executive status. Generally, the executive group was found to be about one percent of the total labor force of a company, although there were variations from company to company in different industry and size categories.

2. Scope of the Survey

To answer satisfactorily the question of how companies handle and adjust to retirement of their executives, considerable information was required. To understand company practices, it was essential to have some idea of the background of facts that determined the evolution of current practices. Differences between practices and policy, where they exist, are important, for they point to the direction in which policies may be undergoing change even before changes are reflected in statements of policy. Of primary significance is the nature of the operating problems that are caused by retirement of executives, as well as the successes or failures in the application of policy to overcome these problems. A long-term view of the company also is needed, for it is only over the long run that a company has had an opportunity to adjust to the retirement problems that have accompanied the steps in its maturity.

To gather this type of information, the study was conducted in three phases, each designed to complement the other in providing information on company experience with executive retirement. First, an extensive questionnaire survey was made among a large and diverse group of companies (referred to in later discussions as the "mail survey"). The second phase of the study was based on intensive field work, conducted through interviews, in a relatively small number of companies (referred to in later discussions as the "field study"). The third phase was made possible through the cooperation of certain companies in the field study group. It entailed gathering, through correspondence with executives who had retired from these companies, their retrospective views about the retirement policies of their former companies, and the impact on the executives themselves.

The mail survey was designed to collect information from a sample of small, medium and large companies, representing all segments of business and industry. Approximately 700 companies were contacted, and 228 supplied full answers to the questionnaire. These companies are diversified by size and industry. The size categories into which the companies fall, according to the number of employees reported, and their distribution among broad industrial classifications are shown in the tabulation below.

In the field study, 46 companies participated, and a total of 156 executives were interviewed, ranging from board chairmen to the lowest level of the executive group, as defined. The companies selected met one or more of the following criteria: (1) they have been successful leaders in their industry for a significant number of years; (2) they recently had a change in their retirement policy or management, so that a before and after view could be obtained; (3) they were in a size or industry category not represented in the group selected by the first two criteria.

From the mail survey, the information gathered pro-

Size and Industry	Number of Companies	
	Mail Survey	Field Study
Size		
Under 1,000 employees....	17	2
1,000–4,999 employees	79	5
5,000–9,999 employees	60	4
10,000 and more employees	72	35
Total	228	46
Industry		
Food and kindred products	23	6
Fabricated metals, electrical and general manufacturing	91	15
Chemicals, petroleum and rubber	41	13
Utilities (electric, gas, transportation, communications)	37	5
Finance, insurance, real estate	29	4
Miscellaneous	7	3
Total	228	46

vided a broad view of existing policies and practices in the retirement of executives in this country. Analysis of the data indicated that the application of retirement policies to executives is fraught with complexities, as evidenced by the varying nature of company policies. The findings suggested questions that should be explored in greater detail and, therefore, provided a basis for a more refined examination of the problems in interviews in the field study companies. In these latter companies, the evolution of their retirement policies was traced, and reactions were obtained on how executive retirement policies had affected operations for which the executive was responsible; how the policies might affect the executive himself; and how the policies appeared to affect other executives and operations. The questions used as a basis for the discussions were as follows:

1. If your company generally observes a mandatory retirement age, what are the most important values received from such a practice?

2. If your company retains executives in employment after they have reached normal retirement age, what are the most important values received from this practice?

3. What problems are faced because of the fact that some executives close to retirement are kept on the payroll although they are not able to perform their assignments as it is believed they should?

4. How does the prospect of an individual executive's retirement influence—
   a. Increasing his pay when there is no change in job?
   b. Granting discretionary bonus, stock option, or other special compensation arrangements?
   c. Selecting, notifying, training and designating his successor?

5. What major changes have occurred in your company's policies and practices in executive retirement in the last ten years?

6. What major problems will be faced by the company in the future if its current practices in retiring executives are continued without change?

7. To minimize the impact of such problems, what general changes in current practice in retiring executives—

    a. Are actually being considered in your company at present?
    b. Could be considered ideal by the company?
    c. Might lead to greater satisfaction among executives?

Through the co-operation of 14 of the field study companies, contacts were made with 205 of their *retired executives*. The retirees were asked to comment on the retirement policies and practices in their former companies and the reasons for them, and to give their reactions, as of the time of their retirement and at the present time. This provided a possible balance to comments made by the *active executive group* from the same companies.

Dealing statistically with the multivariant situations found among the companies would be meaningless, for it is more significant to have an understanding and feeling for the variables in company situations that might reflect different levels of maturation. Further, in a study of retirement, it is also important to be able to evaluate the responses of individuals, for, whether young or old, they have an important stake in and reaction to the retirement practices followed in a company, no matter how objectively they conduct themselves as executives. Thus, the subject required more than a statistical survey, and the intensive field interviews provided the opportunity to interpret the reasons for practices, and any background factors that have tended to condition a company's approach.

In examining the reasons that companies offered for following one particular pattern of retirement rather than another, it became obvious that they are faced with a wide series of problems. The discussion in the following chapters deals with these problems.

CHAPTER II

A Background for Viewing Corporate Experience

Discussions with company executives, including officers, presidents, board members, and chairmen, provided a unique opportunity to search out factors in company history, and problems with executive retirement, which underlie a particular corporation's current retirement practices. During the discussions it was possible to obtain and appraise the reactions of executives to a corporation's policy and to correlate these reactions with age or other personal characteristics that might have been influencing. A general picture of attitudes among the interview group is important to have, since the field study of experience with executive retirement is based almost entirely on what was reported by executives interviewed about company policies, problems and practices.

A. PROFILE OF EXECUTIVES INTERVIEWED

Common to all of the executives interviewed in the course of this study was the articulate manner in which they discussed executive retirement. When one executive said, in speaking of retirement, that "you are working toward it from the moment you are born," he summed up the feeling and awareness of most executives, especially the older men, concerning their own interest in retirement. Throughout the discussions, there was on the part of each of the men interviewed a high degree of involvement with his own retirement and what it would mean to him personally.

Discussions were both philosophic and realistic. In most cases they were specific as well, and were often illustrated with personal observations about events that had taken place, for each retirement in a corporation, among one's peers or at a level close enough so that the executive was acquainted with the individual involved, had been a real and meaningful occurrence. It was strange to find that a retirement referred to as though it had happened only last week or last month had actually taken place years ago. Perhaps this reflects the views expressed repeatedly that executive retirement is part of an organic force. It is tied to a continuing managerial evolution within a company; it is interrelated with the overall staffing and organizational process.

In a majority of cases, those interviewed had been in executive positions for a long enough period to have witnessed some significant retirements, such as the retirement of the founder of a company, of a top scientist or inventor, of someone who had been considered an irreplaceable financial man, or of a chief executive who had steered the company through the trial of the depression years to achieve "unbelievable growth during the forties and fifties." The impact of such a retirement on the corporation, on its current policies, and on the entire executive group was commented on voluntarily by many executives. In each case it was possible to build up a body of common knowledge about a company, its people and its heritage, as known to the several executives interviewed. Moreover, within an organization, differing opinions or additional bits of information from some executives about an experience related by others provided balance and perspective. The views of colleagues, even in fairly large companies, were generally well known; in one company there were repeated warnings concerning "Joe's maverick ideas about executive retirement," and in another that, ". . . the boss wants to make certain changes in retirement for board members."

It might be inferred in viewing executive retirement as part of a long-run process that members of the executive group would be of rather advanced age. This was not found to be the case. In the interviews, individuals were not asked their age, for that question might have hindered discussion or led to discussion of personal rather than corporate problems concerning retirement. But it was most common for an executive to state his age, generally when he stressed the differences in his own views and interests as against what he interpreted as the company's problems and objectives.

Typical statements were: "I am only 44 so I have some time before I have to worry about retirement . . ."; "I am personally knocking at the door at age 59, but . . ."; or "At 64 I've reached the executive scrap heap whether I like it or not." Based on such information, the age of the executives interviewed is estimated to average about 55 years (the actual average age in the mail survey group is 49 years). In all areas of responsibility, including president, sales executive, financial officer, plant manager and personnel executive, every age from 40 to 65 was represented. A few executives were in their 30's. However, the executives interviewed were not intended to represent a cross section of executive ages in a company, but rather of attitudes concerning retirement.

1. Personal Attitudes Toward Retirement

A natural presumption might be that the views and ideas of men about to retire would be a reflection of their ages. Thus, the older a man, the more rigid would be his thinking, the more cantankerous and unreasonable he might be concerning his own retirement, or the more interested he might be in remaining in employment. On the other hand, the younger the man, the more flexible he would be in his views and the more he would be interested in seeing older men removed from active service so as to open up avenues of promotion for himself and his colleagues. These, however, were not the typical reactions. Most of the younger men held older executives in very high esteem, viewing them as persons able to steer and guide, especially when difficult problems arose. These younger men generally deplored the rigidity of formal retirement plans which lead to the forced separation of the more mature executive.

Senior executives generally viewed retirement as an important aspect of company staffing policy, and considered it essential to move older men *out* of the organization and thus make way for younger, more aggressive, more energetic people. Almost universally the attitudes of executives are in conflict with the thesis that the older a man gets the more resistant he is likely to be about his own retirement. The older executive interviewed in the course of this study recognized and accepted the fact that he would be expected to retire somewhere around 65 years of age.

What contributes to acceptance of retirement? In some companies the executives themselves had the answer. They commented that a general conditioning had taken place within the company so that each man knew beyond question of a doubt that his own retirement would occur at age 65.

There was no reason for him to expect any deviation from company policy. The man, his colleagues and his subordinates knew when the retirement date would occur. Preparations had been made for retirement, and the inevitable would have to be accepted.

In a few cases, executives reported that they personally felt they were not able to continue their work assignments, and that they were looking forward to transfer to less demanding work or to retirement. In most of these instances health or personal problems appeared to have had some effect on what they considered to be their own present lack of energy or aggressiveness on the job.

A sizable number of executives, especially in the 45 to 55 age group, expressed a desire to retire early. Some of them were serious about this, but most appeared to view early retirement as an objective which interest in their jobs or more recently acquired financial obligations would never permit them to achieve. One executive, looking back at his earlier idea of retiring before the fixed retirement age, said, "I always meant to take early retirement, but I just never had the time." Those who were serious about early retirement feel that by the time they have reached 55 or some other target age they would have accumulated adequate financial reserves, through personal savings and under the early retirement provisions of the company pension plan, to make retirement feasible financially.

The most common interest in early retirement is for the free time it would afford. Work at the executive level was reported as being very demanding, with the result that sufficient time had not been devoted to family or personal interests that were considered important. In some cases the men were interested in writing, painting or teaching, or in exploring some other vocation that had always been attractive but had never been pursued, such as farming, operating a tool and die shop, or running a ski resort. In several cases interest was expressed in working for a church or some eleemosynary organization.

2. Reactions to Corporate Retirement Policy

Where a company has an established policy specifying a mandatory retirement age, the vast majority of executives had a most interesting reaction to the question, "What are your personal feelings about your company's policy?" While there was complete concurrence with the idea of a normal or mandatory retirement age, there was also almost complete agreement that some other method should eventually be sought to provide for the handling of retirements on a more individualized basis. Many executives in the companies believe that fixed retirement is in the long run best for both the individual and the company. They concede, however, that application of an arbitrary age may result in forcing out some men who are capable and in the retention of some who had lost their verve years before the specified age. It is felt by these men, therefore, that what is needed is a method of determining the age at which a man is no longer able to do his job, for it might be 55 for some, and 75 for others. Several executives hold that if such a formula could be found, it would be in the best interest of companies and the national economy, and that they would support its use in their companies.

Younger executives especially were interested in finding a formula or device that could eliminate the need to choose between the extremes of rigid retirement age practices on the one hand, and total flexibility in the selection of executives for retirement on the other. These men were generally optimistic that systematic and reasonably "scientific" techniques could be developed to make the precise distinctions required to achieve individualized retirement.

Reactions of some young men to a flexible retirement age were, however, that it is feasible to administer such a policy, for they believe that a good manager would know who is doing a good job and who is not. They think retirement could be based entirely on the judgment of a superior, arguing that handling retirements is, after all, no different from handling salary reviews or promotions. What is required is the making of a decision based on carefully developed information. This means information on performance and on medical history. It could also mean getting the advice and counsel of older or more senior executives who may have had opportunities to observe an individual in activities beyond the confines of his immediate work assignments.

A variable approach to retirement is regarded as a sensible objective by a large proportion of executives. They have the impression that people live longer and are healthier than ever before and, that being the case, those who want to and can continue to work and contribute after a fixed retirement age should be permitted to do so. One man summed up his views by saying, "While a fixed retirement age is probably simpler for administrative purposes, the idea of any fixed retirement age being justified in our highly competitive business environment must be rejected, especially as we are all living longer." This view is based on the conviction that to remain competitive, a company must be flexible with respect to both retaining people and retiring them, for only under such circumstances will the organization maintain its vitality and aggressiveness. Comments of this nature were most frequent where people were engaged in scientific or engineering activities, or in highly complicated financial activities within a corporation. Illustrations were cited of older men who had retired but remained active by setting up a home laboratory or office and continuing to do work similar to what they did before retiring.

On balance, however, even those who dissented from application of a mandatory age felt that in the absence of a fairer and more equitable system, compulsory retirement at a given age was probably the best standard. But executive reactions based on matters of longevity and health bring into focus an important aspect of the retirement issue.

B. LONGEVITY AND HEALTH

For the corporation, the finite life span of the individual in comparison to the infinite life span of the corporation underscores the need to plan both for retirement and replacement of executives. The requirements of sound planning exert a pressure toward recognizing an age at which it is presumed that, on the average, a person should retire. Some company policies require retirement at this "average" age; others will permit some flexibility above or below this age based on individual differences. What is this average age and what are the trends in a change in the average?

1. Life Span

Since 1935 and the enactment of social security legislation in the United States, there has been a marked trend toward recognizing age 65 as a normal retirement age, although in many companies there may be no mandatory retirement policy, or if there is, it might be at an age other than 65. Age 65 as a normal retirement age was fairly common in company retirement policies in the early 1930's. After the establishment of the social security system, the drift toward this retirement age continued, and by 1948 company policies overwhelmingly provided for normal retirement at age 65.[5]

In the last several years, sociologists, as well as persons concerned with personnel and with management planning, have felt increasingly that age 65 as a normal retirement age should be reassessed. This view undoubtedly takes into account advancements in medical science and the material increase in life expectancy, especially in the last several decades. It is reasoned that since men who achieve age 65 are far healthier than were their fathers who reached this same age, and since life expectancy is greater today, retirement at age 65 is no longer realistic.

In a sense, arguments about changes in life expectancy are substantiated in fact, but, regarding life expectancy alone, the facts support a conclusion that is far different from what is commonly construed as being the situation. Life expectancy has increased, but the mortality rate for *men* over 60 has not declined appreciably. To understand this, it is necessary to distinguish total life expectancy measured from birth and continued life expectancy beyond age 60. There are more people living longer now than before,[6] but this does not mean that they are living significantly beyond the biblical "three score years and ten."

A male child born in 1954 could expect to live 67 years. Contrast this with the 46-year life expectancy of a child born in 1900. This increase in life expectancy reflects the spectacular advances in medical science and standards of living *as they affect infants*—to an extent that makes infant mortality

[5] Walter J. Couper and Roger Vaughan, *Pension Planning, Experience and Trends,* New York: Industrial Relations Counselors, Inc., 1954, p. 133.
[6] United States Senate Committee on Labor and Public Welfare, *Job Opportunities for Older Workers,* Washington: Government Printing Office, 1957 (Studies of the Aged and Aging, Supplement to Volume IV) p. 2.

relatively uncommon today, as compared with earlier years. This is substantiated by the facts: of 1,000 white male children born at the turn of the century, 133 could be expected to die before their first birthday; while in 1956, only 26 of every 1,000 white male children born in that year did not live to the age of one year.[7]

Mortality rates must be viewed separately for each age group. Mortality is high in infancy and decreases to a minimum at age 10. It rises slowly toward mid-life and then rapidly at the later stages of life.[8] Sharply *declining* mortality rates during the earliest years of life are responsible for the great increase in the number of people who now survive to age 60 and beyond, and account for the fact that the older population of the United States is one of the most rapidly growing sectors of the population.

When one turns, however, to *continued* life expectancy of men over 60, and this group is of concern in corporate executive retirement, the gains in life expectancy have been very small indeed. Despite the progress in the field of medicine since the start of the century, men who in 1900 had reached age 65, had approximately 11.5 more years of life. In 1956, the average life expectancy of a 65-year-old man was 13 years.[9] This is an increase of only one and a half years! This modest increase has been achieved after more than half a century of improvement in the art and practice of medicine and the knowledge of man. On the face of the facts, then, there has not been an appreciable change in the length of

[7] Louis I. Dublin, Alfred J. Lotka, and Mortimer Spiegelman, *Length of Life*, revised edition, New York: The Ronald Press Company, 1949, p. 328, and United States Department of Commerce, Bureau of the Census, *Statistical Abstract of the United States*, Washington: Government Printing Office, 1959, p. 60.

[8] Duklin, Lotka, Spiegelman, *op. cit.*, p. 237.

[9] United States Senate Committee on Labor and Public Welfare, *The Aged and the Aging in the United States, Hearings . . . ,* Part 1, Washington: Government Printing Office, 1959, p. 8.

life for the *average* adult American male. This is significant for executive retirement policy planning. But it is interesting that during the field study many company representatives were impressed with the idea that people are living longer. A comment repeated in almost every company following a mandatory retirement age of 65 was, "Well, maybe age 65 is not the right age and maybe it will have to be moved up to 68 or 70, but we still think it's sound to have a specific retirement age."

2. Health and Aging

Advances in medicine and sanitation have had a substantial influence on the general improvement in health among middle-aged Americans. Attention to diet and preventive medicine, along with a lessening of physical toil, no doubt accounts for the general increase in mental and physical vigor which typifies persons today in the middle and later years.

When considering this improvement, however, against the traditional and historical view of America as a young, vital society, what emerges is a cultural valuation on appearing young. Age appears to have something to do with job progress in corporate situations. It is not unusual to question a promotion on the basis of age. Frequently the question is not age itself but the practicality of promoting an older person into a job where he will not have a sufficient number of years to contribute to the job, or the propriety of promoting a person to a job in which the emphasis is on appearance rather than age.

It is these considerations, perhaps, which prompted several companies to report that there is a subtle fear of aging among some executives because of what it may mean in terms of possible advancement. This may explain why some men are overly concerned and preoccupied with appearance, as one writer pointed out, referring to them as being so "well-fed, well-groomed, and vitamin-dosed, [that] there may be an actual delay-in-transit of the usual physiological decline to partly compensate for lack of psychological growth."[10]

Every indication is, however, that medicine, health and attitudes have combined to make possible a longer, fuller, more productive and more satisfying working life. This is having an influence on company decisions on promotion and may well have a bearing on retirement policies in future years. Company after company uses comprehensive health examinations. Such close, regular attention to health has a cumulative effect throughout the organization. It helps maintain fitness among the executive group and makes the organization alert to the physical condition of individuals. In the later years of working life, individuals tend to be healthier or to understand to a greater degree than ever before their particular health problems. Consequently, they are less of a risk than in previous years when there was no information on executives' health and, therefore, little ability to cope with actual medical problems. It also leads to greater acceptance of older men by the organization, for there is a feeling that specific, comprehensible health problems of executives are not insurmountable.

The discussion above does not establish a basis for anticipating an advance in the retirement age substantially above the typical pattern of 65. However, it does support what is a majority view among the executives interviewed in the course of this study. Executives believe that while a mandatory retirement age, generally at 65, is practical and necessary, it

---

[10] David Riesman, *Individualism Reconsidered and Other Essays,* Glencoe, Illinois, The Free Press, 1954, p. 486.

should not blind a company to the need to examine policy periodically, in order to consider changes in knowledge about aging, the improved health of the older executive group, and the needs of the company. Indeed, probably the most significant research area in this field is concerned with the question, "When is a man *too* old to work?"

C. FORCES CONDITIONING EXECUTIVE RETIREMENT APPROACHES

It is much more difficult to determine the conditioning factors behind current executive retirement practices, considering the influences of health and longevity, than simply to trace the patterns of practices in companies. The formal approaches to retirement that have emerged are often the result of many complicating and elusive forces. A brief review of the background of corporate experience is helpful, therefore, in understanding executive comments on company problems. Experience with formal retirement plans is still relatively slight, because the large majority of such plans are of fairly recent origin. The fixed retirement age emerged as an element of pension plans, and these generally date back to the thirties, with only a small number of plans reaching back before the twenties.

The relatively recent spread of retirement plans has been possible largely because of increased investment in plant and equipment, which has led to great increases in output per man hour worked in industry generally. Higher productivity in all areas of work and in all industries has made possible the support of liberal benefit plans and has provided the means for retirement to nonproductive status of more and more people, from all levels of responsibility.

During the same period that output has increased, business units have grown large and have become heavily staffed. The force of a single personality or of family influence as the decisive factor in corporate survival has dwindled accordingly, and the management organization is now geared to provide a variety of specialized skills in order to meet the demands of change and expansion.

1. Corporate Growth

Patterns of corporate growth have been conditioned by the major factors of war and depression, and of peace and prosperity, which in turn ultimately affect the retirement patterns of a company. War has created shortages of personnel, and depressions have resulted in strange warping of normal employment patterns. Peace insures orderly personnel planning, and extended periods of prosperity cause growth of corporate structures beyond that normally anticipated, creating the challenge of finding more and more capable people to lead expanding enterprises.

Growth is, of course, also conditioned by market and technological forces, so that there are times in an industry when one company spurts ahead, while others are achieving more moderate expansion. Illustrations of this are to be found in the spectacular growth during the decades of the thirties, forties and fifties of companies producing automobiles and such related products as rubber. Contrast companies in those industries with, for example, many companies in the food processing industry which, generally, achieved their present structure earlier and, except for mergers, have evidenced steady rather than spectacular growth. Similarly, in insurance and finance there has been growth, but again this has reflected general economic developments or public demands, rather

than the effects of new scientific or technological developments, as has occurred in the expanded chemicals industry,
for example.

The growth and size of modern corporations made the
problems of staffing more complicated than had been the
case in the smaller organizations of the past. Growth underscores the need for a more orderly approach to the transfer
of responsibility upon the retirement of each older genera-
tion of executives, especially in the case of founding fathers
of a corporation. Viewing the experience of the companies
in this study specifically, there is little question that a major
impetus toward the formalization of retirement practices has been corporate growth, which in turn stimulated
the introduction of formal pension plans and the establishment of a normal retirement age. The brief review below
of specific cases in company experience indicates the significant role of pension plans in facilitating application of formal
retirement policies. These cases also typify the historical
factors in company situations that have shaped retirement
patterns.

2. Role of Pension Plans

Pension plans have generally emerged in companies
that have found it possible, and often necessary, to establish
such plans as their operations increased in size and reached
a relatively sound financial position. Financial stability makes
it feasible to set aside significant sums of money with which
to provide a proportion of income for employees upon retirement. Frequently, instituting a retirement plan has been a
matter of a company competing with other employers in
terms of fringe benefits as well as salaries, in order to attract
employees, including executives, to the company. In other

cases, providing pensions for employees has been viewed as a normal part of a sound employee relations program or has resulted from wartime control of salary increases. But for whatever reason the pension plan is introduced, a normal retirement age, at least for actuarial purposes, is established. This sparks and stimulates the establishment of that age as the customary retirement age.

It is quite clear from reviewing company histories that systematic approaches to retirement actually did occur with the establishment of their pension plans. These plans were generally instituted when a company was in a position to afford them, or could not afford not to have them in terms of recruiting and retaining personnel, or because of pressures from unions, especially after the United States Supreme Court ruled that pensions were a legitimate area for collective bargaining. In considering the historical evolution toward formal retirement policies there are striking similarities in company experience. Companies have had to relax the application of a specified retirement age because of manpower shortages during wartime. Where plans were established in companies prior to World War I, it took them considerably longer to reinstate the customary retirement age because of the absence in this earlier period of any general industry practice respecting retirement.

a. Experience Under Older Pension Plans: Typical of the practices and experience of several companies in the survey group is the case of a company that introduced its formal retirement plan about 1910. Under this early plan, age 70 was considered to be the terminal age for employment. The plan permitted early retirement at age 60, but subject to completion of 20 years of service. However, because retirement benefits were related to career earnings, retirement more usually took place nearer to or at age 70.

With World War I, the company found that a shortage of good personnel at the technician and executive levels was creating manpower problems, and the formal retirement plan was relaxed with respect to the mandatory retirement age. This suspension remained in effect through 1925 because "employees had become *accustomed* to working beyond age 70." But by 1925, it became apparent that a more systematic and formal approach would have to be taken to retirement, because of long-run staffing problems and a lopsided age distribution among employees in important segments of the organization. In that year, the company established age 65 as the retirement age to become effective by 1930.

In effect, the organization was given five years to adjust to mandatory retirement at age 65, for the plan operated in such a manner as to lower the retirement age by one year annually, until 65 was reached in 1930. Because of the number of superannuated employees, however, it was not always possible to adjust to the new mandatory retirement age in as systematic a manner as was anticipated. Thus, during the five-year adjustment period it was necessary to stagger retirements and in some cases to permit men to stay for a year or two longer, or, in other cases, to require that a man be forced out although he had not reached the then current retirement age. During this period, the company provided discretionary pensions to take care of those whose pension was adversely affected by the imposition of the formalized mandatory retirement age policy.

The dropping of the retirement age year by year, in order to finally arrive in practice at the retirement age established under the policy, has been followed rather widely. Almost all of the field survey companies took this course, regardless of when a fixed retirement age was first made effective.

b. Experience Under Later Pension Plans: The experience related above has had its parallel in at least a dozen other companies where the pension plan and retirement age was first instituted in more recent times. In one of these companies, the mandatory retirement policy had been made effective originally in 1937, but many exceptions had been made to the retirement age of 65 in those earlier years. By 1942, wartime personnel shortages made themselves felt and the policy was set aside until after the war. In 1946, the policy of retirement at age 65 was re-established, and it took only three years to return to the application of mandatory retirement. While other companies with roughly the same experience were not able to return to the mandatory retirement age immediately upon the end of the war, a majority of the companies that relaxed their formal retirement age policy during World War II had reinstated it by the time of the Korean crisis in late 1950.

Apparently, in the companies where a retirement program was started at some time in the late thirties and it was necessary to relax policy during World War II, a return to the original policy following the war was achieved more quickly. No pronounced deviations have occurred in the policy approaches of these companies since that time, undoubtedly because no single outside factor has been found disruptive enough to require a short-run modification of retirement policy.

In some of these companies with more recently established plans, the executives interviewed were familiar with the reactions of executives at the time the then new plan was introduced. Usually there was considerable resistance by executives to the imposition of formal, mandatory retirement. One executive speculated that, even though the president of his company thought it wise to establish a mandatory retirement age, it would never have stuck were it not for the existence of the pension plan, which specified a retirement age to which mandatory retirement could be tied. Since the company was providing a significant portion of the contribution for pensions, this made retirement attractive to the executive group in a way that it otherwise would not have been.

3. Effect of the Business Cycle

In some companies economic factors outside the company situation have caused particular problems in the handling of retirements, particularly in recent years. An example of this is a company in which a merger, prior to the depression of the thirties, brought into the company a large number of executives. The addition of these executives to the original group distorted what was considered to be a normal age distribution of executives for the size of the particular organization. In order to protect job tenure during the depression, the company hired only a few young men for executive positions in those years. With the war in the forties, recruitment was again curtailed and executives were held on in active jobs after reaching retirement age.

Upon the end of the war, the company faced serious staffing problems at the executive level, because of the advanced age of the top executive group, and the hiatus in age and experience between this group and lower levels of management. A merger after the war with a company in the same industry, in which employment and retirement experience had paralleled that of the company under review, added to the problem and led to an overabundance of personnel, especially of older employees. But the company's mandatory retirement age was 70; and the only course available to the company to overcome its problem of personnel imbalance was to stimulate early retirements, which was accomplished by substantially improving the pension benefits available to employees who selected early retirement. This, however, involved great cost to the company. In recent years, changes in the pension plan permit and make attractive early retirement at age 65, which today is the normal retirement age, although 70 is still the terminal age.

4. Family Influence

In a relatively small company in the survey group, family interests have been rather dominant in the evolution of the company's fortunes. In past years it was difficult to imagine forcing a member of the family in ownership into retirement, but evolutionary factors have changed this. Because of the necessity to keep abreast of going practices, a formal pension plan was instituted in this company in 1943, but no mandatory retirement age was adopted at that time, although it was anticipated that normally employees would retire at 65. While many did so, just as many did not. By 1950, a second factor came into play. The company was growing, diversifying its activities, and the need for a larger management team became apparent. At a point, it was clear that a flexible approach in the handling of retirements, at both the executive and other levels of the organization, was threatening to cause future staffing problems.

The company felt that for growth and development it would be important to slowly but systematically move toward requiring retirement at age 65. Today, there are few deviations from mandatory retirement at that age, although they still occur. In each instance, exceptions are permitted only where they are in the best interests of the company. Sometimes members of the family are excepted, because they are still active and important in the company, although not as influential as they had been in the past; in other instances, exceptions are made in cases of specialists or other important executives who have directed growth or expansion in important areas of the company's business.

5. Influence of a Founder

In one company, as with several others in the study, its striking growth was achieved during the lifetime of the men who today are the chief officers of the company. There is a desire in this company to treat deferentially and more favorably those executives who have steered and guided the company over the period when growth was achieved through the development of new products, the creation of an effective organization, and the acquisition of capital. This company presents an interesting profile of a large company attempting to adjust to the demands for system and orderliness which appear to be imposed upon larger organizations. A normal retirement age is followed which tends to be effected for most employees, including executives, unless they have been with the company for two decades or so—representing its period of greatest growth. There is a tendency to make major exceptions to policy for the executives who themselves have made the major policy decisions. One executive in this company commented that "these men tend to view themselves as somewhat indispensable, but, in effect, they are not, and they recognize this; and that is their problem in resolving a formal retirement plan in terms of what they would like to do for themselves."

* * *

From this review of executive reactions and the background factors that enter into systematized executive retirement policies, it is clear that the particular situation of companies, over given periods, has largely conditioned the approaches taken in the retirement of executives. Also apparent is a general recognition among executives of the arbitrariness of mandatory retirement, although it is acknowledged as a most effective administrative tool. This background is useful for consideration of company practices in applying a retirement policy to the executive group, as examined in subsequent chapters.

CHAPTER III

Retirement Policy and Executive Staffing

FORMAL RETIREMENT POLICIES PROVIDE a basis for planning in advance to deal with the retirement of executives when they reach an advanced age. The existence of such policy also calls attention to the need for arranging for the orderly and systematic transfer of responsibility at the time each executive retires. Thus, the incidence of retirements is closely related to staffing of the executive organization. Each retirement has multiple effects throughout an organization, as responsibilities of younger men are shifted in order to fill voids created by the retirement of older, experienced men. This impact that retirements have on an organization is seen best by considering the reasons companies offer for following their particular retirement policy.

Many factors are cited as important in the establishment of a corporate retirement policy, and some of these emerge out of the history and environmental situation of companies, as discussed in the previous chapter. This chapter sets forth the classic arguments companies offer in support of either mandatory retirement of executives or a flexible approach in the handling of executive retirement. The discussion is based on comments from representatives of companies in both the mail and field survey, who pointed out the specific problems and other factors in their companies that have determined the respective executive retirement approaches.

The advantages and disadvantages of the two major retirement policies are discussed below, with no attempt at this point to reconcile seemingly contradictory points of view. Before turning to this discussion, a few terms must be drawn into focus, for they are pertinent to the discussion here and throughout this report. While the meaning of the terms may appear clear on the surface, historical use in some company situations, or the influence of terminology in insured pension plans, may have given them differing shades of meaning.

1. *Normal retirement age* refers to the age that has been established at which a person is expected to and generally retires whether under a rigid or flexible retirement policy. It is generally the retirement age specified in pension plans.

2. *Fixed, mandatory, or compulsory retirement age* refers to the age that has been established beyond which persons shall not be retained in employment. In some cases a company specifies a normal retirement age that is congruent with the mandatory age; in other cases normal and mandatory retirement ages are different; for example, age 65 may be set as the normal retirement age, but age 70 may be the mandatory age for retirement.

3. *Flexible retirement* refers to a situation where the time for retirement is determined on an individual basis, by

taking into account differences in the ability of individuals to continue in their jobs.

A. MANDATORY RETIREMENT POLICIES

Mandatory retirement is, by far, the major policy approach of the companies represented in this study. Of 225 companies in the mail survey group (three did not report their policy) and the 46 companies in the field study group, 222, or about 82 percent, have a policy of mandatory retirement at a fixed age. These 222 companies account for 86 percent of the approximately 4.8 million persons employed by the companies participating in this study, and their executive organizations together number about 42,000 persons. In the discussion that follows, an amalgam of the advantages of a policy of fixed retirement age, as seen by executives in companies in a variety of industries and in varying size categories, is presented. Obviously, no one company necessarily finds all of the advantages listed; nor is it to be inferred that statements by company representatives about the advantages of setting and adhering to a mandatory retirement age necessarily mean that this practice is actually followed in their respective companies.

1. Facilitation of Orderly Company Planning

A fixed, mandatory retirement policy is generally regarded by executives as being easiest to integrate with over-all company programs—including training and replacement plans, retirement benefits and other financial matters. Many companies, moreover, take an over-all view of retirement and see it as the final step in a process of manpower management, which includes recruitment, training and development, promotion and, eventually, retirement. Thus, each phase of the development and progress of an executive in a company, including his retirement, is related to total personnel and management planning. Companies that integrate retirement policy with staffing report that they must know with a high degree of precision when executive retirements will occur. Each retirement is seen as sparking a chain reaction throughout the executive organization, and eventually requiring the recruitment of new individuals at the entry level of employment for managerial skills. One company reported that 150 promotions resulted from the retirement of one man.

Companies which have adopted mandatory retirement because it facilitates sound company planning fall into two extreme categories, based on size. First, there are the large companies which may employ thousands of managers. In those companies, simply by nature of their size, the magnitude of the personnel and financial planning problem makes it an absolute necessity to take a long look and careful approach to promotions, transfers, replacements and financial arrangements attendant upon retirement of executives. In such companies it would be chaotic to attempt to deal with retirement on a case-by-case basis. Careful planning permits the companies to integrate retirement with promotions following on the training and development of younger able men from all parts of a company. Insurance and pension liability will have been calculated to an extent that permits the setting aside of definite foreseeable amounts annually.

The precision with which a company can approach its handling of retirement under a mandatory retirement age policy may becloud the practical problems which occur with some frequency. Regardless of planning, there always exists the possibility that individuals may move to another company or seek early retirement, or that the inroads of death prior to retirement can distort a planned program of executive promotion, replacement and retirement. Some companies have found that fortuitous events have greatly disturbed their planned promotional moves. But where the executive group is especially large, size alone can provide a degree of flexibility which permits coverage of executive openings that occur through unexpected developments which remove men from the executive role. Companies which have been in this situation have found that, generally, alternative arrangements can be made reasonably quickly because of the scope and nature of the executive development and staffing program.

The second category of companies which see mandatory retirement as an aid in planning is comprised of smaller firms. There are distinct similarities in views about mandatory retirement between these and the larger companies. In the small companies there is a great reliance on the unique contribution of an individual, and it is not possible to engage in broad, comprehensive planning as in larger organizations. Even in many of these smaller companies, however, it is reported that there is merit in attempting to devise a plan for executive succession and then modifying this plan as may prove to be necessary by uncontrollable circumstances. Executives in these companies feel that without a plan for systematic training and replacement the corporation would not be in a position to adjust to the loss of an important executive. Preplanning serves to build up considerable knowledge of available skills and opinions and judgments on the optimum allocation of those skills.

2. Automatic Changes in Leadership

A company policy specifying that a man must relinquish his authority and retire from work upon attaining a specific age inevitably results in a regular, foreseeable change in leadership. This was cited most often as one of the factors which has prompted companies to adopt a policy calling for retirement at a fixed age. In many companies the feeling exists that without such a policy it would have been difficult to have asked a particularly successful executive to retire at what might have been a normal rather than a mandatory retirement age. In many instances it was pointed out that even though the retired executive had been highly successful on the job, and at first it seemed that the company's loss upon his retirement was a deep one, his successor, more often than not, brought something to the job—new values, new viewpoints, new skills, greater drive. Perhaps it was a new spirit of creativity, a burst of energy, or ideas for expansion into new market areas or products. But given change, a sizable number of companies reported that they are better off today because of the retirement of an older man than they would have been had the retiree been permitted to stay in office.

Frequently this revitalization process was also referred to in terms of gaining new skills and talents, especially in those activities or industries where a particularly high value is placed today on technological knowledge and skill. Revitalization of the executive staff also appears to have an effect "down the line," for effective changes in executive staffing spur new thinking and stimulate new action throughout an organization. This appeared to be the case in heavy manufacturing, where research and development have been assuming more and more significance. It was also the case in electrical and electronic activities, where it was reported that the absence of mandatory retirement would have hindered a company's ability to recruit new men who could understand and deal with new problems effectively, not only for top jobs but throughout the organization.

3. Incentive for Young Executives

One of the most frequently cited advantages of mandatory retirement is a corollary of the principle that such a policy provides automatic changes in leadership. Mandatory retirement may provide an additional incentive for younger executives to join and stay with a company. The argument is that where retirement is mandatory at a specified age, each person in the executive hierarchy stands a far better chance of achieving a promotion and of obtaining a higher skilled, better paid job than if a superior were permitted to stay on until he was no longer able to function.

Many companies in the field study group had found it valuable to cite their policy of executive retirement at a fixed age in the recruitment of new and younger executive employees, particularly among those with professional or scientific training. In attracting such personnel, recruiters feel that stressing a mandatory retirement policy establishes a presumption of certainty of promotion leading to greater responsibility earlier in life and at almost a foreseeable time. Moreover, fixed retirement is presumed to guarantee job security for executives, and companies report that when there is such security, executives appear to be willing to transfer responsibility progressively before retirement. Too frequently, however, this has resulted in a younger man being given additional responsibility in his current role, but it may not be commensurate with his authority.

It is interesting to observe, however, that some executives in companies following a mandatory retirement policy feel that it has a depressing effect on executive motivation. These executives depreciate the value of moving men step by step through the executive hierarchy and into retirement. It is their belief that if a man is not certain about his progression up the executive ladder he will try harder for recognition, be more aggressive, and therefore be more effective as an executive.

4. Improvement in Management Relations

Noteworthy among the reasons cited for fixed, mandatory retirement is that it provides an opportunity for the establishment of better relations between junior and senior men. In several instances, a mandatory retirement policy had been introduced recently. In these cases it was recounted that in the "old" days, senior executives hoarded job knowledge and refused to share information and know-how even when it was apparent that they would soon be retiring. But with a fixed retirement policy there is no question of an older man staying on, and there is no reason for him to be overly protective of his job knowledge and business contacts. With a formal retirement plan containing a specific retirement age, the fear of retirement might persist but the executive knows that he will be retired and much of his job-oriented resistance vanishes.

The hoarding of job skills and knowledge is not the only aspect of the problem. If an executive does not understand that he must retire, he may attempt to delay retirement, sometimes as a result of not training a potential successor. Where it is clear, however, that company policy will force retirement, there is no possibility of dodging the executive responsibility of communicating to his successor information concerning the more subtle aspects of the job, and in every way helping the new incumbent to be fully prepared.

5. Advantages for the Retiring Executive

Proponents of mandatory retirement at a fixed age feel that in addition to the many advantages of such a policy for the corporation there are real values for the individual executives, as follows:

1. When an individual knows that retirement will occur at a specific time it is possible for him to prepare himself and his family, not only financially, but emotionally and socially for the impact of retirement. This does not mean that an executive *will* plan, but he is *on notice* to do so. Firm adherence to specific retirement dates for all executives continually reaffirms to others approaching retirement age the fact that retirement will occur on schedule for every executive, and this is part of an important long-run conditioning process that eventually gets built into the fabric of organizational practice. To the extent that such conditioning is successful—and with respect to many companies this was observed to be the case—individual executives are encouraged to prepare for their retirement.

2. It is felt by many companies that fixed retirement removes individual anxieties over when a company will determine that the individual is no longer qualified to stay in his job. Many executives referred to this in terms of preserving individual dignity. If, through retirement policy, one man's career is concluded while another is permitted to stay on the job, this may mean that the retiree loses his self-esteem or his dignity among his peers or his social status in his community. Formal retirement at a fixed age for all means that, whatever the age may be, each person is treated equally and on an objective rather than subjective basis.

3. Fixed and mandatory retirement which results in the termination of men who are still able and capable of working enables them to find outlets for their energies and abilities in other types of work situations. Thus, retirees who are productive and energetic do not clog up promotional lines by staying on the job. For they can, once retired, engage elsewhere in productive work for pay or on a volunteer basis.

4. Fixed mandatory retirement is viewed by some as providing compensation for a lifetime of service in the form of leisure time. When a man has worked for a corporation for 30 or perhaps even 40 years, he has not had time to enjoy outside interests. Retirement, as some suggest, provides the opportunity to travel, fish, or spend time telling stories to grandchildren.

B. FLEXIBLE RETIREMENT APPROACHES

In some companies, flexible retirement is a matter of policy; in others, it is the absence of policy which has resulted in flexible retirement practices. Only 13 of the reporting companies now follow the extremely flexible practice of handling all retirements on an individual basis. Another 36 companies have established a normal retirement age, at which it is common for most executives to retire, though not all do so. Companies in both groups find distinct advantages in the practices they follow. The advantages cited in dealing with retirement on a flexible basis are discussed below.

1. Sound Manpower Utilization

Where retirement is flexible, a company is able to retain an individual indefinitely, so long as he can do an effective job for his company. This is viewed by companies as most rewarding for the individual, most profitable for the company, and most economical for the nation. Considering retirement as an individualized process would appear therefore to be far sounder, in terms of utilizing human resources, than a mandatory retirement approach calling for the retirement of men at an arbitarary age, who, though retired, could still have made a significant contribution toward achievement of corporate goals.

There is a general feeling on the part of executives, even in many companies following a mandatory retirement policy, that it is not entirely fair to equate capacity and ability with chronological age. While companies with a flexible policy find it advantageous to retain older men, companies following the mandatory approach consider that it is impossible to deal with retirement as a business, management, or individual matter in the absence of an arbitrarily established mandatory retirement age.

On the other hand, companies following a flexible practice start from the concept of equity to the individual and the need to use rare resources; they take the position that a company shirks its responsibility when it refuses to make a decision about an employee. Deciding when a man should retire is not essentially different from other personnel decisions, although there is a greater degree of finality in the retirement decisions. Representatives in these companies ask whether it is possible for management to avoid making decisions about people throughout their careers. Since they feel that it is not, they conclude that it is hypocritical or irresponsible to find ways of avoiding the making of individualized decisions about when a man should retire.

Equating capacity and ability with chronological age, in such a way as to determine retirement age, is central to a discussion of retirement and the corporation. To the extent that capable executives are lost, a loss is suffered by all. Thus, in companies that take a flexible approach, it is frequently argued that broad national economic considerations alone dictate against mandatory retirement and support the flexible approach. Executives in these companies strongly urge that individual decisions be made about when to retire an executive and that such decisions can be made by alert management, with a degree of objectiveness which should distinguish all management actions in dealing with people.

2. Benefit of Mature Men

Unlike most jobs in the organization, the executive function is frequently described as one which requires the exercise of judgment, wisdom and fair play in planning, organizing and directing major sectors of the enterprise, rather than specific job knowledge alone. The development and ripening of these abilities comes with time and after long exposure to operating problems. Older executives have experience, status and personal contacts. They offer a company a pattern of action based on experience, and a consistency and dependability which may be relied on and which might not be achieved when younger persons are placed in important executive positions. Moreover, the older experienced executive has a status among his peers within the organization as well as in the community or industry at large. Such status may be important to the effectiveness of a manager, and it probably could not be readily matched by a younger man.

In those companies which follow a practice of flexible retirement, many situations were cited where a variety of considerations had made it necessary for older men to be relieved of operating responsibility. Sometimes it was a matter of an individual's health, the need to expose younger men to operations, or to develop men for anticipated corporate growth. Where this has occurred, companies often find it more valuable to permit the older executive to devote his time and capacities to long-range planning and policy development. It is felt that in the long run these endeavors pay off in terms of corporate growth and in the development of younger men.

3. Continuity of Management

Assuring continuity in executive positions can be difficult because of company growth, development of new products, death, terminations, etc., according to the experience of the companies in this survey. Thus, despite the scope, extent or completeness of executive staff planning, it is impossible to take account of all exigencies. A policy permitting a man to be retained even though he has reached normal retirement age is a necessary escape valve. Adjusting the date of retirement to actual executive personnel needs can insure smooth transition and avoid abrupt breaks in management continuity.

A variety of situations can be imagined where a company does not have replacements available at the time an executive retires. In young companies the demands for experienced leadership might be great. Older companies which have experienced tremendous growth in recent years, surpassing anticipated levels, also might need experienced leadership beyond that available through the ordinary developmental process. Perhaps turnover has occurred as men were attracted from one company to another. These are all situations where mandatory retirement could mean an abrupt change in a corporation's leadership and which many companies feel can be handled best only through a flexible retirement policy.

4. Training of Junior Executives

Permitting a man to stay on in his job so long as he is contributing to the goals of the enterprise provides a more prolonged period for the training of potential successors, because it is geared to the needs of the job and not to the arbitrariness of a retirement date. Frequently, for top jobs in the organization this is a particularly troublesome matter, because it is so difficult to know exactly how to train or develop a man for a top job, or when a replacement is ready for the job. By retaining senior executives, they are in a position not only to coach younger executives but to give them advice and counsel as they progressively take on operating responsibility. This seasoning of younger executives over a period considered necessary is viewed as a way of maintaining a sound corporate executive structure and an integration and continuity of leadership that would not otherwise be possible.

5. Improvement of Morale

Job security, even at the executive level, is believed by a substantial number of executives to do more for morale than any other single matter. They claim that, when an executive is doing his job well and feels secure in his job, regardless of his age, his morale is far higher than when he faces a fixed retirement date. Executives in companies with flexible retirement policies reported they felt that the older executive has considerably more security in their companies than in companies following mandatory practices. It is also felt that high morale in the senior ranks has a constructive influence on the morale of subordinates.

6. Improvement of Retirement Benefits

It is obvious that where company pension plans permit benefit credits against earnings after the normal retirement date, retirement incomes can be improved to the extent that service is continued beyond that date. Since pension benefits are related directly to earnings and length of service, this can be an important factor in companies where executive pensions are geared to career earnings and where higher salary levels are reached rather late in a man's working life. Thus, in those situations where lengthening out an individual's career would improve his pension benefits, there is greater pressure by an older man to continue in employment. In companies with flexible retirement practices, and which provide pensions based on career earnings, there has been a considerably greater tendency to permit an executive to continue working and thus improve his retirement benefit. This advantage of a flexible retirement approach does not obtain, of course, in companies that do not permit the accumulation of pension credits for employment beyond the specified normal retirement age.

7. The Factor of Adaptability

Flexible retirement practices provide a company with the opportunity to adjust to a variety of situations which may arise out of changes in the competitive situation, shortage in manpower, or new operating problems. At the normal retirement age a valuable executive may be moved out of the position he occupies but retained in company service as a consultant. Having no line responsibility and being familiar with the company and its problems, he can then be both objective and informed in his judgment. The consultant role is not only a method of retaining executive skills, if they are needed, but it also shelters such skills if there is any fear that after retirement a person who has been in a key position might accept work with a competitor, thereby causing embarrassment for the company.

8. Personal Considerations

For that group of individuals who are so attached to their work and who become so adjusted to working life that retirement could prove a hardship, flexible retirement provides an opportunity to continue with a pattern of life that is at once constructive and meaningful. Men in this situation are not faced with the problem that occurs in those companies where a fixed retirement policy cuts a man off from a world which has been the major factor in his life for over two, three, or perhaps four decades. Obviously, the significance of work varies from individual to individual, but it is especially among the executive group that one would be likely to find a high percentage of individuals who feel the urgent need to continue to be busy and creative and to contribute to the productive process.

C. IMPLICATIONS OF POLICY

It is impressive to find that companies, in citing the advantages of supporting a particular pattern of executive retirement, place so heavy an emphasis on the relationship between the retirement of executives and the staffing of the management organization. Companies with a mandatory retirement policy stress the importance of that approach in facilitating orderly company planning in staffing an organization. On the other side, companies which follow a flexible policy, find it advantageous to have flexibility in handling retirement because of uncertainty about future staffing needs in their companies.

This matter of relationship between retirement and staffing has two facets. The claim is made in companies with a mandatory retirement policy that compulsory retirement at a fixed age is a stimulus to the training and development of younger executives, for the fact of retirement creates the imperative for such preparation. In companies where retirements are handled with some degree of flexibility, the advantage cited is that executives can be retained selectively, beyond what is considered as the normal retirement age, and are available to guide their younger successors and smooth their orientation in jobs with responsibilities that are new to them. But within the companies that take these two approaches, not all executives agree with their company's policy. An older vice president of a company that has a mandatory retirement policy, which is adhered to rigidly, stated that "training can go only so far and then experience must take over." Is this true? Is only limited success possible with the training and development of men for executive responsibility, and is it to be anticipated that application of a mandatory age may undermine organizational staffing patterns? This executive obviously felt that this is so.

Contrast this view with that of another executive in a company that has a policy of mandatory retirement at a specified age, but which is frequently violated. He stated that "executive development and retirement are tied together, and for the plans and systems to work, they must both be used. The fact that they [the company] don't retire older people is what's wrong with retirement in this company and what makes executive development inoperative. If people retired on schedule, there would be more training and development and a systematic approach in designating successors."

It is interesting that regardless of the particular approach to retirement the advantages cited are invariably in the interest of effective management staffing, although the concept of how staffing interests are served differs. Proponents of a mandatory policy hold that in the absence of a fixed retirement age, training and development do not occur with the precision that obtains where retirement policy dictates termination at some specific date in the future. Companies following a flexible policy feel that it is desirable to retain a predecessor until the younger incumbent has demonstrated his ability to deal with all aspects of his responsibility.

The reasons for differences in approach among the companies are, of course, determined in large part by factors beyond the confines of the logic of one approach or another, for company background and other environmental factors often come into play. To understand the reasons for particular patterns of action in companies, it is necessary to consider their experience. These experiences are discussed in later chapters, and actual company practices are reviewed and contrasted with their stated policy. Variations between practice and policy, as they emerge, signify the compelling factors that cause departures from stated policy.

CHAPTER IV

Central Problems in Applying Retirement Policy

S YSTEMATIC RETIREMENT POLICY contributes to sound, long-range organizational planning, for it forces a company to prepare for management succession—an immutable fact of organizational life. Planning for succession requires periodic review of executive performance, which may result in promotion or salary adjustments. On the other hand, some executives may be passed over, and this can have multiple effects on executive morale and motivation.

In this chapter the influence of retirement on executive performance, morale and motivation is considered. Company actions in maintaining an effective management organization have a self-perpetuating influence on the organization and on executives well before any single individual reaches retirement age. Thus, each executive is constantly made aware of his own aging and eventual retirement, and of the standards of executive efficiency a company expects.

A. EXECUTIVE PERFORMANCE

The selection and screening processes through which executives move at every step in their working careers should filter out individuals whose work performance and potential does not meet the standards the company wishes to maintain. Variations in patterns of performance among executives are to be expected, and typically they become more pronounced with age. Individual differences presumably arise to some extent from personal factors which influence a man's desire or ability to attend to or maintain interest in his work. They are also, however, the result of factors in the work environment. While no attempt was made to probe into the personal aspects of executive life as they might condition job performance, it was clear that performance of older men is a function of both personal and work factors.

Each company in the study was asked to report on the performance of older executives in terms of: "What problems are faced because of the fact that some executives close to retirement are kept on the payroll although they are no longer able to perform their assignments as it is believed that they should?" Experience in the two groups of companies varied. Only about a half of the mail survey companies answered this question, and their responses were as follows:

Evaluation of Performance	Companies
No poor performance problem........	74
Poor performance problem	45
Not serious 39	
Serious 5	
Affects morale 1	
Total	119

Although 45 of the reporting mail survey companies indicate they have a problem with poor performance among the executive group, only five feel it is a serious problem. One company stated that the problem of poor executive performance has been its bad effects on the morale of employees generally, including executives. Of the 45 companies reporting a performance problem, 31 estimated the percentage of executives who are poor performers. These estimates are of course only rough indicators of the extent of the problem, since the basis for evaluating performance probably differs among companies: in five companies, less than 1 percent of the older executives are poor performers; in four companies, less than 2 percent; in three companies, less than 4 percent; in two companies, less than 5 percent; and in one company, less than 8 percent. In 16 companies it was simply reported that a "few" were not performing as the company would like.

This experience is in direct contrast to that found among the field study companies. Only 10 of the field study companies have had no problem with poor executive performance. Of the 46 companies in this group, 31 reported that poor performance among older executives is a significant problem. Five other companies recognized that poor performance existed but regarded it as not serious. Where the problem has been pronounced, companies stress that poor performance on the part of executives is far more significant than when found among employees at lower levels of the organization and that poor performance at higher levels of management can be a test of the resourcefulness of a management, in terms of finding ways of dealing with the problem.

In the field study companies, the seriousness of poor executive performance is related more to the level of the executive hierarchy at which it occurs than to the number of executives involved. In fact, it was difficult for most executives interviewed to quantify the number of cases of poor performance, especially because of differences among the cases and in their significance as a corporate problem. The president of a fairly large company commented on the matter to this effect: "There may be only one person in this company among all of the executives who is not doing his job the way it should be done. This would be less than 1 percent of the total executive group. In terms of numbers, therefore, the problem is not a big one, but if I am the man who is not effective, this company could really be in trouble." Certainly, in making this comment, the president was not impressed with his own importance, but rather with the relationship between the poor performer and the locus of the decision-making function in an organization. To the extent that the poor performer is insulated from making significant decisions, he represents a calculated cost rather than a calculated risk to the company.

1. The "Nonperformers"

The field study companies reporting the existence of poor performers in their executive organization referred to this as a problem of "executive deadwood," a phrase that gives cognizance to lack of motivation at the executive level. It was used to describe situations of poor executive performance as evidenced by a loss of interest in work or a tendency to "coast through to retirement." Generally, the executives referred to were men in their late fifties and sixties, although some were younger. Most were, however, men who had made a particular contribution to the company, through special or devoted service over a long period of time. These factors gave them a form of security in their job that is looked on throughout an organization as inviolate job tenure.

While the problem of executive deadwood varied among the companies in extent, it appeared to occur more frequently, or at least was recognized more readily, in companies that have established a mandatory retirement age than in companies where retirement of executives is handled with some flexibility. Moreover, companies with the problem of poor executive performance were generally those in which recruitment into executive jobs from outside the company is not typical, because of a high degree of career employment based on executive promotion from within.

The discussions of executive performance during the field study were quite significant, because awareness of the poor performers differed with the rank of the man being interviewed. The higher the rank, the more likely an executive felt poor performance to be a problem in his company. There were instances where men two or three steps removed from the highest level of management reported that no such problem existed, while men in higher ranking positions considered executive deadwood to be a significant problem. Differences in views stem partly from occupational isolation or a form of executive provincialism. A marketing man may understand the work of a colleague in manufacturing but the likelihood is that he cannot appraise it. Presumably, however, a man somewhat higher up would have a clearer picture of the performance of both men in terms of their contribution to executive teamwork in achieving the over-all objectives of the company.

In commenting on the reason for the lack of precision in evaluating executive performance in his company, a president observed that he was at fault, for he had not communicated effectively with his staff and officers over the years. As a result they did not have a clear picture of job objectives, so that their evaluation of executive performance differed from his.

This man felt that some of his subordinates were coasting because they do not really know what is expected of them. In another company, an executive vice president was struggling with methods of evaluating executive performance. His problem was that his own ratings of executives once removed from him differed from the ratings of their immediate superiors. This executive's evaluations of performance showed deadwood to be a problem while other ratings did not. The experiences of these two executives are cited because both found and were disturbed by a divergence between the performance they expect of a good executive and that which satisfied lower ranking executives in their respective companies.

Generally, the ineffective executive is identified by such signs as not keeping up in his field and having lost interest in his work, which limits ability for growth. Cases of this sort present real problems for a corporation; generally the individuals had performed satisfactorily in past jobs over a period of long and conscientious service, and it would be difficult for a company to terminate them or force their early retirement. In many instances the problem of inadequate performance was not of a man's making but that of his company, for he had been promoted beyond his level of ability. In some cases the men fell short of expectations when they could not keep pace with the changes that had occurred in company products or services or with deeper changes in the structure of the industry or market in which the company operates.

This matter of dealing with a man who does not have the capacity of growing with his job is of great concern to executives in many companies, especially as they see for future years further innovations in operations, marketing, distribution and internal administration. Sometimes contemplated changes have been delayed or indefinitely postponed because of the resistance of men who are a "deadwood" problem. Even where a change has been finally introduced, the process has been slowed up by the need to condition and convince a few men who are no longer really able or capable to meet new challenges in their jobs.

2. Case Examples of Company Experience With Older Executives

Two illustrations drawn from company experience typify the problems that arise because of what is referred to as executive deadwood, or poor executive performance. One concerns a single executive; the other, a group of executives. A third case shows how an older executive can continue to contribute significantly to company progress.

Case 1. This company had a recent problem in its attempts to introduce a highly advanced data processing system. The difficulties began shortly after World War II, when the company recognized a need for better and more timely information on which to base important corporate decisions. All company-wide record-keeping systems at that time fell under the purview of the chief financial officer. He was described in the course of the field visit as a career employee who had moved up within the organization after "many years of constant and valuable service." His primary promotions occurred during the period immediately following World War II, which was a time of great expansion for the company.

There was a general belief in the company after the war that a punched card system would provide more efficiently the kind of information needed. The chief financial officer insisted that punched card record-keeping systems would not necessarily produce savings in over-all clerical costs and, moreover, great problems and long delays could occur in the event of machine breakdown. With delays in studying this administrative matter, other divisions of the company threatened to introduce their own systems if the financial department would not. It was only then that this executive agreed to recruit the personnel needed to plan and introduce the more modern system, and it was not actually installed until 1951.

Within the last two years, almost the same problem has repeated itself. There was interest in integrating various phases of accounting, sales and inventory records, through the use of high-speed electronic computers, to provide management with important information for operational, financial and marketing decisions. The financial officer again resisted the introduction of an integrated system. As a consequence, the machine record unit was separated from the financial department, and today it is a separate staff department providing service to every division and department within the corporation and using the most modern high speed equipment, to the advantage of the company.

In this case, the financial officer's resistance to change frustrated management in the achievement of company objectives. He evidently never had the training, knowledge and vision needed for his job at the time he was promoted, but he had been promoted in the absence of available capable men. It was difficult for him to grow with the times. The fact that he had to be constantly pushed into accepting change, rather than exercising leadership, limited his contribution to company progress. His attitudes induced time-consuming and costly delays for the organization.

Case 2. The problem in another company is indirectly related to technological improvement. In this company—a most prominent one in its industry—the management had been exposed to severe labor problems over the years. Negotiations with union representatives had been typified by the retreat of plant managers in the face of strike threats on important issues. As a result, the company's collective bargaining agreements had become cluttered with a number of contract clauses which restricted management in reorganizing jobs and work assignments, and in introducing new methods and equipment.

Early in the 1950's it became apparent that if the company was to survive and meet growing competition from other companies in the industry and from abroad, it would have to take a more vigorous stand in dealing with the union. Plant management, however, had demonstrated to the union in past negotiations that it would yield to union demands under the pressure of bargaining and withdraw management demands for changes in the collective agreement. It was felt, therefore, that it would be difficult for the company to take a firmer position in negotiations.

Top management, faced with such softness on the part of operating management, was perplexed, yet felt it was imperative to check the union and press its own demands. Accordingly, the company took a lengthy strike, but it succeeded in eliminating some of the restrictions in its collective bargaining agreements. Upon the end of the strike, the company turned to an evaluation of the management team. Drastic changes were made in plant manager assignments, based on the ability of the individual to operate a tighter, more efficient organization, and to introduce and make effective changes in methods. The company did not overlook managerial weakness which had led to past problems, for, in many instances, early retirement was forced on some managers. This permitted a restaffing of the management organization with men who recognized and were able to deal with the operational problems faced, even where it required a showdown with a union.

The problem in this company was quite serious, for many individuals were involved and the production process was widely affected. The plant managers demonstrated they were not able to cope with the demands of the changing times. Obviously, some of the men involved had reached a plateau in terms of their personal abilities. In other cases men may have lost interest in their jobs because they had been in them for so long; they found it difficult to change their customary approaches. Health deterioration also may have drained from some of these executives the vitality required to meet demanding responsibilities, and family difficulties may have diverted the attention of others from their long-range job responsibilities.

Both cases described above illustrate the types of problems that arise for companies as executives advance in age and lose the drive that would move them to accept change as a challenge and to discard outmoded managerial patterns as new circumstances dictate. Although these cases are representative of many situations among the field study companies, it was far more common to find cases in which older individuals in the executive hierarchy were energetically moving with the times. It is in order, therefore, to also illustrate with a case of this kind.

Case 3. On the day one company in the field study group was visited, the president of the company was reported to be unexpectedly out of town and unavailable for interview. He and a subordinate executive were involved in announcing the introduction of a new product. The subordinate executive had been, for almost half a decade, in charge of developing the new product and working out arrangements for its financing, manufacturing, and distribution. His task had been most difficult, because of early resistance to the new product within the company, and later resistance from outside the company when it was necessary to raise capital for its development.

The successful launching of the product was viewed as a great personal triumph for the man who was primarily responsible for having had the vision and determination to do what had to be done. This man had passed the company's normal retirement age of 65 some years ago. Chronological age had not interfered with his being an effective executive in the years prior to and after age 65. Other companies in the study reported similar, although not so timely, illustrations of imagination, vitality and perseverance in their older executives. It is clear from such cases that aging does not inevitably result in an inability to meet executive responsibilities.

B. COMPENSATION AND PROMOTION

It has been indicated that poor performance among older executives is sometimes a problem for a company. However, this problem does not occur inevitably among executives. Most executives sustain high levels of performance under the pressure of their assignments, or as they move up in an organization, and they expect to receive recognition for their performance, regardless of their age. But, as men advance in age, is it in the interests of a company to continue to increase their compensation or offer them promotional opportunities? The discussion below deals with company practices respecting salary treatment, other forms of compensation, and promotions for older executives.

1. Salary Practices

Of the 228 mail survey companies, only 150 provided information on whether salary increases are routinely granted to older executives. In 68 of these, age has no influence on salary increases in the years prior to a man's retirement. In 41, increases are permitted, but only when there is evidence of special merit. In the remaining companies, salary increases are either not provided or are limited: in 17, increases are not provided unless a man has a change in job; in 13, there is a gradual leveling off of salary in later years; in 9, increases are normally not granted in the later years; in 2, increases are sometimes granted to raise a man's pension.

Among the field study companies, far more detailed information was made available. The large majority of the companies in this group, 41 of the 46, allow salary increases to men in executive jobs, regardless of their age, but three reported that the increases were not always earned. Two of these three companies report an interesting problem that has arisen because of an unwritten policy restricting salary increases after an executive has reached age 60, unless exceptional merit is involved. In both companies experience has been similar. Each time a name is passed over as salary recommendations are presented, there is a tendency to go back and reconsider the performance of the executive who has been passed over, in an effort to find some exceptional accomplishment. It was readily admitted at the top corporate level that merely in raising the question, there was a tendency to create a basis for salary increase. Thus, an older executive generally gets his increase and, because of a peculiar reverse reaction, it sometimes is more than younger executives receive.

Variations in corporate salary policies create differences, of course, in practices with respect to salary increases. Some companies carefully follow a defined salary schedule for men in the managerial and executive ranks, although in many companies salary ranges are not controlling. Where they are, however, many older executives were reported to have reached the top of their salary range long before they reach age 60. In such cases, the evaluation of company practices respecting salary increases for older men must take into account the location of an executive's salary in the range for his job. Many executives have reached the top of their ranges and are no longer receiving salary increases in the five years or so before retirement. However, this situation arises because of the mechanics of salary administration, for these companies do not intend, as a matter of policy, to prohibit or restrict salary increases because of age. Where policy has restricted or salary schedules have limited pay raises, company policy often provides for regular cost-of-living increases.

In another, though relatively small, group of companies, salary increases are handled differently. An *officer* is provided with a salary increase budget of a specific number of dollars, to be distributed as he sees fit among the men within his area of responsibility, although proposed increases are generally cleared with higher authority. Here the matter of whether an executive would be provided with an increase if he were an older man would obviously vary with the executive making the decisions about specific increases. Generally, older men appear to be more inclined to provide salary increases for older executives, while younger men tend to increase the compensation of younger subordinates.

One executive's justification for giving first consideration to deserving younger men, in the distribution of his budget, was that they are the men whom the corporation must retain and provide with incentives to do a more creative and imaginative job. He frankly admitted that this meant he frequently passed over older men in order to provide more attractive increases for younger executives. In contrast, another executive feels that by providing salary increases to older executives he is able to motivate older men and stimulate them to make significant contributions to the company in the years immediately before their retirement.

In one company salary increases are not provided after a man reaches age 60 as a matter of policy. The company adopted this policy because it is convinced that job performance drops dramatically at about that age. In still another company there is ordinarily no salary increase after age 60, because the company's pension plan is based on average earnings over the final 10 years of employment. Salary increases during the last few years of employment can be costly, for they inflate an executive's retirement income and thus increase the long-term liability. Three companies viewed the salary increases granted late in a man's career as a form of "good-by payments." In one company the "good-by payment" was designed simply to provide a single amount to an individual in his last year of work prior to retirement. Because of income taxes, this company viewed this payment as a morale booster rather than of actual benefit to the individual.

In about 15 percent of the field study companies, there were executives who reported that, in their own and other departments of their companies, salary increases have been granted to individuals approaching retirement in order to "beef up" their retirement benefits. The retirement plans of these companies are based on some final earnings formula (such as the average of the final five years' earnings, or the highest five of the final 10), instead of on career earnings.

In companies with such plans, substantial increases in pay late in a man's career can be significant in determining the amount of his pension. This has been such a problem in one company that the controller considers it one of his important responsibilities to police salary increases, especially during the last five years prior to a man's normal retirement age. He exerts pressure on responsible executives to review what he considers "outlandish" salary increases, and in many cases salary recommendations are reconsidered and scaled down.

2. Other Forms of Compensation

Restricted stock option and discretionary bonus plans have become features of executive compensation plans in many companies. For that reason, the answer to the question of how age affects executive compensation is answered only in part by considering changes in salary alone. A fourth of the field study companies provide restricted stock options for executives. Under these plans, qualified executives may exercise options open to them during a period depending on the terms of the option plan of the particular company, which may run up to 10 years after the option has been granted (five years is most common in this group of companies). Typically, the companies permit options to be granted only through ages 60, most commonly, and 62 and 63, less frequently.

Age limitations in granting stock options derive from the formula under which options are granted and exercised, and from a company's desire to achieve orderly retirements. It might be impractical to grant an employee an option any time after he has reached his 63d birthday, considering the period of time which must pass before an option may be exercised, and because of possible market developments. To obtain maximum tax benefits, an option usually must be exercised within 90 days of an employee's termination of service, except in case of death.

On the company's part, there is a general reluctance to let an open-end stock option run for too long a period. From the employee's standpoint, a longer period of time provides him the opportunity to wait out market movements until it is attractive to exercise his options. Company representatives pointed out that if options could be exercised without limitation related to the normal retirement age, there would be pressure from executives to remain in employment beyond that age if stock market conditions at the normal retirement age were unfavorable. Since policy-level executives participate in the plans, pressure could be exerted to violate the specified age for retirement.

Several companies that specify age 65 for retirement do not grant options beyond an employee's 60th year, and require them to be exercised within five years. These companies feel that their option plan is related to the company's formal retirement plan and supports the terminal age of 65. The reason is that by requiring options to be exercised within five years and by ceasing to grant options after age 60, the option program for the individual and his service with the company terminate at the same time. Additionally, some companies report that options granted to younger men provide an incentive to performance not always achieved among older executives.

The discretionary bonus is more difficult to report on than restricted stock option programs. Typically, among the companies studied, an individual's age does not affect his participation in a bonus arrangement, even though a company's policy might restrict salary increases after age 60.

Bonus payments are most frequently deferred until retirement, but in a few cases they are paid immediately. The only variation to be found in company practice was among the companies which pay the bonus annually. These companies do not restrict participation of older executives in the plan, but may defer the granting of the bonus during the last five years of employment until after retirement.

Many companies with executive bonus plans make a real effort to relate the bonus to individual job performance. In many areas of responsibility, this was done through examination of profit and loss statements on a departmental or divisional basis, maintenance or improvement of staff services, increases in sales, and the like. However, it was readily admitted by some executives that it is difficult to determine variations in executive performance with precision, and this has resulted in the distribution of bonuses among executives according to fairly arbitrary formulas, based primarily on salary and responsibility, but not on age.

3. Promotions

The extent to which age is a factor in determining salary increases and other forms of compensation for executives is slight by comparison with the influence age has on executive promotions. In almost every company in the field study group, attention is given to the age of men being considered for promotion within the executive hierarchy. It was obvious in almost every company that the promotional process was not viewed as a method of rewarding men for service. Instead, promotions are seen as the mechanism for insuring that assignments important to the perpetuation of the enterprise are staffed with capable men. Consequently, the chain of promotion that might be assumed to lead from one job to another frequently had been broken, and younger men had been promoted over older men.

It was not unusual for executives with broad responsibility to indicate that it is unlikely one or another of their subordinates would be promoted after a certain age. But that "certain age" varied not only from company to company but also from department to department and from job to job. A summation of age-job-promotion relationships may help in seeing the corporate problem. The points made are drawn from comments of executives interviewed rather than from precise experience in their companies. They may, therefore, be considered as indicators of what these individuals would do under given circumstances, rather than what they have done.

1. The higher up a man is in the organization the more time he needs in his job to initiate and complete important programs and developments. This was stated almost as a natural law. From this flowed a corollary observation concerning the chief executive position. The older the present chief executive of a company, the more likely that his successor will be a much younger man. This, of course, occurs in part because men who grew up in a company with the president will be retiring about the same time or shortly after the president has reached retirement age. Thus, there is no contemporary or near contemporary available to remain as president for a period of years. There are companies, of course, which require a period of service as an officer before promotion to the presidency—perhaps 10 or even 20 years.

2. While the same conditions prevail with respect to positions subordinate to the presidency, more variations may be anticipated. One of the most common of these is that the longer a man who is being retired has been in a top job, the more likely that an interim appointment will be necessary

before the post is filled for the long term, and it is also likely that this interim appointee will be an older man. The reason for this is that a man who has been in a job for a long period of time usually has outlived the people who have been "standing in line waiting to take over the job." The available men are, therefore, second or third stringers. In many cases they are too young, and have not worked close to the retiring boss. An older executive, even a man in his sixties, may therefore be promoted with the prime objective of developing a successor. This situation could arise at the presidential level, but generally it does not, because of a relationship usually established between a president and his board of directors.

3. The more specialized the job, especially if it is a staff assignment, the more likely is the promotion of an older man to fill such a vacancy. An older man can be quite readily replaced with another specialist, upon his retirement, for in specialty areas much less time is needed for training or "breaking in," than for positions directly concerned with operations.

From the comments above emerges a concept of promotions as an instrument of organizational planning rather than a morale booster. In this light, promotion policy may be seen as undermining morale, especially among older men, as they come to see no possibility of promotion. They may be passed over as early as 10 or 15 years before they reach the company's mandatory retirement age. It is important, therefore, to consider the views of executives in relation to corporate practices as they affect the morale and motivation of older executives.

C. MAINTAINING MOTIVATION AND MORALE

Executives in the field study group accept the idea that the success of the corporation rests in large part on the abilities and motivation of the executive group. The men at the top set the direction and tone of the organization and make the major decisions that affect their company's position in the market place. Thus, the continued motivation of these men toward high-level performance is crucial to success. As to whether motivation requires high morale, or whether high morale is indeed important, executives might disagree, but the majority tend to the idea that the two are inseparable. Given the importance attributed to high motivation among the executive group, it is understandable why the men interviewed felt so strongly about the problem of "executive deadwood," and about preventing any further compounding of the problem.

In discussing motivation, company representatives frequently offered a definition of necessary executive attributes. According to these definitions, an executive is a man who is aggressive, energetic, inventive and incisive. He can not only plan and direct work but can also motivate others in doing the job he wants done. Against this concept, many executives are regarded in their companies as having once had the specified characteristics, but they have been lost or become dulled at some point in the individuals' long period of service in the organization.

There is a pattern among the field study companies of individual executives having remained in a specific area of responsibility for long periods of time. Apparently this is true of industry at large. According to a recent report on the job history of top executives, 1,700 men in that particular study group entered their present jobs at about 50 years of age, "after long service, and a certain amount of standing around waiting for their predecessors to move up or out."[11] And many executives contacted in this study expressed the view that to stand around and wait for a promotion has a deadening impact on both an individual and his organization; especially since a promotion might never come. In a number of cases it was reported that men had entered a company and moved fairly rapidly through the organization early in their careers. But so frequently these men reached a plateau—sometimes by age 50, sometimes later. This flattening out of the career curve is generally attributed in companies to one or more of the following factors:

1. A man may reach the optimum development of his capabilities and can not progress further within the organization.

2. There are a limited number of positions in the executive organization, or the organization is overstaffed and cannot offer continued promotion to its employees.

3. An organization is shrinking or not growing as fast as it had earlier, so that promotional opportunities are no longer available.

4. The higher in the organization a man moves, the more important both ability and personality become; team relationships with other executives point up inadequacies never observed before.

5. A man's age, relative to others, may be such that in the organization's best interest it has to promote another man in giving cognizance to long-term staffing.

6. Because of health or other reasons, a man may no longer show himself as a vigorous, energetic executive.

[11] "1,700 Top Executives," *Fortune*, November, 1959, p. 138.

What action do companies take in dealing with executives whose performance is substandard, and to what extent is such action successful? Only 133 of the mail survey companies gave information on this point, and they reported one or a combination of four types of action, when an executive falls off in his performance: (1) he may be transferred into new or different areas of work assignments, on the presumption that a new job will provide new challenges and, therefore, stimulate his interest in work and motivate him to greater effort; (2) he may be aided in dealing with his responsibilities by assigning to him a subordinate or an assistant who has the characteristics the company feels are important; (3) he may be terminated—through early retirement under the provisions of a company pension plan, or disability retirement where a health problem exists; (4) he may be given a special assignment or an advisory role within the organization, thereby removing him from direct administrative responsibility.

The discussions in the field study companies permitted executives to explore their own thinking about poor performance as they had encountered it, and to reflect on the several problem with which they had dealt. Underlying the comments of almost all of these company representatives is a recognition of the fact that almost every action taken with respect to an individual executive has a direct impact on the morale and motivation of all executives. Thus, company action is usually carefully considered in the light of the particular circumstances prevailing in each company situation, and thought is given to developing the right atmosphere for an action which must be taken. Companies employ a variety of techniques, as outlined below, in their endeavor to maintain a vigorous executive organization.

1. *Appraisal of performance.* Most executives stressed the

importance of fair appraisals of executive performance in maintaining a basis for executive motivation. These evaluations provide a measuring rod for executive performance and an opportunity for uncovering deadwood or other problems that exist or are coming into being. Evaluations also serve to notify all members of the executive group of performance problems, so that if overt management action becomes necessary, it could be justified on the basis of facts.

While almost every executive stressed the importance of sound appraisals of performance, almost as many felt that no single appraisal system they knew of was as effective in doing the job as they would like. Some companies have elaborate punched-card systems which record fine details of executive background and performance in a variety of terms; some of these numerically record evaluations of personal characteristics as a basis for computing an evaluation score for individual executives. Still others take a less mechanistic approach and have attempted to evaluate performance in terms of an executive's ability to define his objectives and achieve them in a given period of time; these companies regard such accomplishments as the most important measure of executive performance.

A unique feature of some executive evaluations is appraising how well a man makes presentations before committees of the board of directors, in addition to observing his performance on the job. During these presentations, men are questioned rather carefully about operational methods, new activities, financial performance, etc. Their ability to handle themselves well under questioning provides clues as to their continued ability to perform. These board presentations also serve to establish an understanding among officer-executives about the performance of other men on the executive staff. Thus, when some drastic action is taken against poor performers, such as forcing them to retire, the basis for company action is generally well understood.

One company reported that there is no problem at the very top levels of the organization in maintaining high levels of motivation for the individual executive. The men who had been chosen for the critical jobs could be called "self-starters." They are men who find their motivation from within themselves, rather than through "carrot on a stick" stimuli provided by their immediate boss. However, at levels immediately below this top level, the management recognizes a problem. Most frequently, personal problems have reduced the efficiency of individuals. But, in part, the company has contributed to the problem. As explained, evaluations of executives vary with the times. In good times, when income is high and the market is sound, a company is most likely to overlook deficiencies and retain men even though they are not performing effectively, since there is no pressure to examine the financial liability that may be entailed. In periods of business recession, however, the justification for retaining the nonperformer becomes difficult. Appraisals then become more critical, as the company's financial situation throws the light of scrutiny on ineffective executives.

Intensive evaluation of the executive organization in terms of its structure and staff is frequently stimulated by change or other pressure. Sometimes it is a change in company administration, as a new chief executive takes a fresh look at his staff. In one company several of its top officers, including the president, had recently retired at about the same time. This company's earlier practice of permitting men to stay on after normal retirement age was the cause of so many key executives having reached retirement age in close succession. The new president established a retirement policy calling for retirement at normal retirement age without exception. He also pursued a vigorous program of forcing the early retirement of selected older executives, for he judged it important to replace them with younger men so as to get an age balance in the executive organization.

In forcing retirements, the company made every effort to explain how important such action was to the present and future efficiency of the organization. Liberal financial arrangements were made, and no man stood to suffer because of his retirement. Nevertheless, a high degree of restiveness developed on the part of a majority of executives over age 55, who viewed their situation as precarious because they were carryovers from the previous administration. This uncertainty over their status and future, and conjectures as to whether they too would be selected for retirement, seriously impaired the effectiveness of the management team. Probably because the organization was highly decentralized, there was a lack of understanding of the over-all problem and corporate needs.

Another company had a similar problem. Extremely flexible retirement practices of the past had led to a generally older executive group. Moreover, the more efficient men felt no urge to work hard themselves merely to support executive deadwood. In fear of destroying morale, nothing was done about the situation until it became apparent that corporate survival demanded action, and the company then moved to separate older executives. In this case, separation of older men and poor performers improved morale and was a stimulant to remaining executives. It opened new promotional opportunities and motivated men of ability, ". . . to take audacious action." Three other companies reported similar experience. In each of these companies a very close relationship exists among executives at corporate headquarters, which made for free discussion of the problem. Consequently, the executives who remained understood the need and reason for separations.

2. *Job rotation and transfer.* Many company manage-

ments feel that a major factor in poor executive performance is that a man becomes frustrated in his job as he views his future. The thought of continuing in the job he has already had for some years is depressing and leads to his poor performance. Such companies follow a fairly consistent pattern of rotating executive and managerial personnel. New assignments are believed to be more attractive only by virtue of the fact that they are different, and the rotation practice serves both motivation and developmental purposes. Company experience with rotation of executives is generally favorable, although transfers alone do not solve all of the problems a company may face in dealing with ineffective executives.

In one company, the possibility of transfer is explored whenever early retirements are requested by a superior for an executive or manager who has had long service with the company. The case is reviewed by the top industrial relations executive who discusses the proposed retirement with the superior executive and with the potential retiree. The point made to the man's superior usually is, in substance: "There must be some job that this man can do, otherwise why has he been retained in employment for so long?" Frequently this question has induced suggestions for using the individual in wholly different areas of work, with gratifying results.

A case cited in this company was that of a chief engineer who was no longer performing satisfactorily in his assignment. At a point in his career early retirement was proposed. Through exploration, it was discovered that work could be made available for the engineer in which his training would be an asset, and today the former chief engineer is in charge of maintenance and plant facilities at the company's chief manufacturing center. An interesting sidelight was the fact that although the former engineer was willing to accept his new assignment, his superior-to-be was not willing to accept him, but was forced to. At the time of the field study the individual in question had just reached age 65 and his current boss, who was so worried at the outset, now feels that this man is irreplaceable and that the company should permit him to stay beyond his normal retirement age.

Despite examples of successful transfer, some executives hold that there is no satisfactory way to handle men at the executive level who are no longer effective in their jobs. One company has attempted transferring men, but without success. Demotions have typically not been satisfactory. The establishment of assistant positions as a means of sharing job responsibilities has proved costly, and demoralizing to both the assistant and the executive. It is felt, therefore, that in dealing with poor executive performance decisions should be based on cost. If it costs more to retain the individual in his present assignment than to transfer him, he should be transferred. If it costs more to keep him in any job than to retire him, he should be retired.

Some companies have attempted to deal with ineffectiveness in line executives by transferring them from field or plant operations to a staff job. Executives so transferred frequently have even more problems than if they had remained on their former jobs. The reason offered for this was that in a plant or field job an executive operates to meet fairly clearcut standards, whether they be profit and loss statements or production records. He is in a position to judge his own performance by watching the figures on the income statement or production report. However, the staff man has no convenient measure through which this can be done. Lacking such a device, the field man in a staff job tends to fall completely apart.

3. *The "soft sell."* In the large majority of the field study companies, it is usual practice for the superior of an executive

who is not performing as he should to have an informal talk with him, in order to stimulate and interest him to a greater extent in his work. This is generally a "soft sell" approach, taken during lunch or while a man is on a business trip with his superior. The result often is good, since such discussions can and do lead to uncovering a problem that can be disposed of. When an informal talk is not successful, discussions are held with the individual, as part of the formal appraisal of performance, so as to establish a basis on which to transfer a man laterally, with the idea that a new job will provide new challenges to stimulate his performance. If transfer is not successful, termination may follow, and this pattern becomes understood throughout the executive hierarchy.

4. *Stimulus of the bonus.* In a company in which marketing accomplishments are stressed in executive evaluation, the experience has been that an executive who is not effective in his job tends to identify himself unmistakably. Any substantial error in making a decision in the marketing phases of the company's operation is readily recognized and results in the modification of, or withholding of, a year-end bonus. This serves notice to the individual that his performance has been unsatisfactory. Should he continue to fail to measure up, he usually can anticipate forced early retirement.

When all other actions fail, it may be in the best interests of a company to demote or terminate an individual. Such actions can have a salutary effect on the management of the company, as already illustrated. In several of the companies studied, a demotion is often camouflaged as a job transfer, but even so, unfortunate reactions can result. An extreme case occurred in a company that effected such a "transfer." The executive concerned had voluntarily chosen early retirement after his "transfer," which he obviously recognized to be a demotion. Once retired, he insisted in a series of public statements, in a community in which the company operates, that he had been forced out by his company. Such circuitous company actions were felt to be unavoidable in some cases, but were considered by many of the men with whom this matter was discussed as demonstrating the need to consider the "dignity of the executive" in whatever action the company decided on, whether it be transfer, demotion or retirement.

CHAPTER V

Interaction of Retirement Policy and Executive Succession

E XECUTIVES INTERVIEWED in the course of this study considered future retirements as creating management issues of central importance. The retirement of older men leads to a recurring series of staffing decisions and shapes plans for development and succession at the executive level. How do companies achieve planned executive succession and how are these plans affected or influenced by retirement? Is it, as one executive observed with respect to his own company, that success in finding suitable replacements for retirees and in effecting smooth transfers of responsibility has occurred "not because of superior planning, but because of good luck?"

No majority practice was found among the companies studied in dealing with the retirement-succession cycle. Instead, wide differences were found in company practices and policies—usually related to company size, corporate structure, or the types of jobs in question. However, companies generally have not left these matters to chance or luck. In fact, the inroads of retirement on executive staffing have made vivid the interaction between retirement policy and succession at the executive level, and have led to the introduction of elaborate programs to assure perpetuation of an effective executive organization.

A. ADVANCE PLANNING FOR EXECUTIVE SUCCESSION

In companies with an established normal retirement age, especially where it is mandatory, there is strong opinion that future manpower needs can be anticipated and planned for more definitely than when the retirement age varies. The normal retirement age calls attention to future retirements and therefore stimulates action toward identifying and preparing replacements. However, planning for succession and identifying potential successors also takes place in companies with a flexible retirement age policy.

Many companies give recognition to the need to plan for succession by establishing a formal program for management inventory and development. Such programs are designed to identify the strengths and weaknesses in the existing management organization, as a basis for building on the strengths and overcoming the weaknesses. They also enable top management to evaluate at any time the state of preparedness in an organization for finding replacements, as vacancies occur through retirement, death or other causes. This relationship between retirement policy and training and developmental programs that are designed to assure executive succession, is a most important one, and is illustrated by two examples.

One company was clearly assisted by its executive development plan in handling executive retirements in a systematic, routine fashion. This company introduced its plan in the early 1950's, but it was almost five years before the plan was accepted by some in line management as being effective. Before the plan was installed, executives with divisional responsibility had repeatedly pressed for and succeeded in retaining, beyond normal retirement age, men who were considered to be still capable. As the developmental program passed through its earlier stages, however, and proved to be more and more effective, the top executives began to see and understand the relationship between retirement and succession and the importance of planning and development. They began to accept the idea of a normal retirement age, they were prepared for it, and the organization was prepared for the retirement of executives. Thus, it became possible for the company to hold to its normal retirement age and for retirements to occur systematically—something that had not been the practice in past years.

In the second company, the chief executive, following what has become a fairly common practice in industry at large, stressed his reliance on the preplanned movement of men within the executive organization. The plan in his company is based on detailed descriptions of all management positions, supplemented by information as to the possible advancement of each executive, his age and his retirement date. A listing is also made of possible successors for each position, along with the steps to be taken to prepare men for vacancies that will be created by retirement. This coordination between retirements and executive succession is highlighted on "staffing charts" by the use of color codes against those positions which will be vacated within three years by men scheduled for retirement.

The major difficulties encountered by companies in planning for retirement of executives fall into two groups.

The first concerns the precise identification of successors, the methods to be used in developing them, and the achievement of a smooth transition when an executive succeeds to a position upon the retirement of another man. The second is related to the position itself, which may not be static but may be undergoing change prior to the retirement of an older man or after his retirement.

1. Identification of Successors

Several distinct methods are used by the companies studied to find men capable of succeeding to positions in the executive organization. Obviously, more than one method may be used in a company, depending on its size and the personalities of the men involved. Four of these methods are sufficiently common to warrant discussion, although two others—the use of an outside consultant and special committees of the board—were also cited.

1. *Decisions by the chief executive.* In several companies it is not unusual for the president or chairman of the board to, alone, designate those who will be developed for future promotion. This pattern of action is typical in smaller companies, where the chief executive officer is either a significant shareholder of the corporation or has firsthand knowledge of the abilities of individuals; he might even have been involved in their initial selection. However, the same practice prevails in several fairly large corporations.

When the chief executive has a deep understanding of the problems of a company and a broad knowledge of his staff, he is in an excellent position to identify and place men in jobs they can perform best. But selection by one person can be dangerous, and some illustrations of difficulties with this approach were provided among the field study companies. Generally these arose where the chief executive gave attention to personal characteristics, with little or no attempt to isolate and evaluate the capabilities and characteristics needed in specific positions.

In one company, where it was readily admitted that promotions are made in the judgment of the president alone, executives feel that the practice has introduced some confusion into the management organization. Executives responsible for major operations could do little to plan for systematic succession upon the retirement of older executives within their departments. In some instances a successor had not been appointed to a position for periods of up to two months after a man had retired. This problem has existed at all levels of management. However, there is no indication that the personal approach has been damaging to company interests, since the company has been and continues to be highly successful and well regarded in its industry. Perhaps the reason for this was given by an executive in the company when he said, in substance, that "the boss understands our company so much better than his staff, we can't even see the objectives he is striving for in his staffing arrangements, and maybe our only problem is we resent that the boss is generally right."

2. *Delegation of responsibility.* A method companies frequently use in the development of successors for managerial positions is to assign to each executive full responsibility for the development of his replacement. The president is responsible for planning for the development and training of his successor, each vice president for his successor, and so on throughout the executive organization. The rationale behind this approach is that planning for managerial succession is a primary responsibility of every executive. So important and crucial is this responsibility considered, that several companies in evaluating the performance of an executive place

great emphasis on what the man has done to train and develop his successor.

Some years ago, the president of one company was faced with the need to find a successor for his job. Both the president and the board of directors had decided that no one in the company's executive group was capable of succeeding to the top executive position. An executive search found one capable person, but he was then president of a smaller company and was not interested in leaving it. However, through a merger with that company, the new man was brought into the organization and today he is president; the former president has moved to the board chairmanship.

3. *Centralized referral systems.* Several examples were found among the field study companies of situations where, either by virtue of company size or decentralization over a broad geographical area, it had become necessary to develop and maintain a centralized inventory of the talents, abilities and experience of managerial and executive staffs. These inventories form the basis for appraising the current situation with respect to executive succession. They are maintained at company headquarters, where men are selected for referral to vacancies, as they occur, anywhere in the management organization.

Such programs are frequently referred to in companies as executive inventory or identification programs, because their objectives include the identification of potential managers on the bases of education and experience, recorded evaluations of performance and/or results of various psychological tests. Companies with these programs generally have available punched-card and data processing equipment, through which it has been possible to relate the inventory of available talent to the retirement of executives on a year-by-year basis, projected over future years. This correlation of available talents and future staffing requirements permits a company to review and evaluate its manpower situation several years ahead, and thus avert possible crises.

One company cited an illustration of how the system had operated in the case of an individual who had reached the normal retirement age shortly before the field visit. Executives within the organization had once felt that it would be necessary to go outside the company to replace the retiring executive, because of the nature of his specialization. But three years before, the inventory system had identified a man with the requisite training and other qualifications for which the company was looking, who then worked in one of the smaller outlying plants of the company. He was brought to the headquarters office and exposed to broader training and developmental activities and closer evaluation. Thus, he was prepared for and took over the responsibilities of the older man upon his retirement.

Other companies have found that an identification program has been helpful where particular problems have arisen because of company expansion. Several cases were cited of finding men to fill positions in new offices in foreign locations where fluency in a specific language was needed. This may not appear to be a retirement matter, but in some situations transfers of this sort have disrupted preplanned correlation of promotional moves with openings anticipated through retirement. The existence of the management inventory system, however, provided the needed flexibility to adjust to the unexpected vacancies, by enabling the management to quickly locate men capable of moving up in the executive hierarchy. This is another illustration of the relationship between retirement and over-all staffing.

4. *Review by the board of directors*. Three of the field study companies have an established procedure for exposing

executives to appraisal by their board of directors. Arranging for review of executives by a board may be more easily achieved in companies with inside directors or where a number of directors are also officers of the company. The advantage of this procedure is that it permits directors to become acquainted with the men and their abilities and, thus, when vacancies occur in top jobs, it is possible to consider realistically promotions from among the executive staff. In one of the companies an individual identified by the board as having the makings of a top management man is given special assignments and problems to work out and report back to the board. His performance on these assignments provides an opportunity to gauge the man's ability to take responsibility, lead a project, analyze and evaluate findings and make effective recommendations.

2. Influence of Job Factors

The nature of job responsibilities tends to affect company views on planning for succession and the amount of lead time that is necessary before designating and announcing a successor. In general, it appears that men engaged in engineering, accounting or scientific activities require less training and development for more responsible positions in these areas of specialization than men in line or staff positions who are moving up to a higher level of responsibility. This bears out a general presumption that where the nature of the work rests heavily on knowledge in a professional field, the man who has been professionally trained can move into a new job and take hold more easily than one who is promoted to a position calling for the exercise of general management functions.

In companies producing capital goods, top sales positions

were viewed as among the most important in the corporate organization. In these companies, it was reported that retirement from these positions created particular problems for the organization. A top sales executive has generally established highly personal relationships with customers, and in many instances it is difficult for a company to replace such a man who has been particularly successful. In a division of a national company which manufactures heavy industrial equipment, the top sales executive was personally responsible for selling some of the largest equipment installations made by the company. This executive was retired at the normal retirement age, but customer reaction threatened a possible loss of business, and forced the company to rehire the man on a part-time basis.

However, many other companies have found the transition of responsibility from one sales executive to another to be a minimal problem. This experience derives from the nature of the product market involved. In a company that produces a wide range of products, no one sale or customer has a particularly determining effect on the over-all sales picture of the concern. Each unit of sale in and of itself is rather small and the loss of one unit is generally balanced by the development of new market areas and the acquisition of other customers. Even in situations where the product market is not fragmented, it was reported that the retirement of sales executives has not been a problem. The explanation given was that, while a retiring sales executive may have one group of contacts, his successor usually has some contacts, and soon develops others. More often than not, the new man retains some proportion of his predecessor's customers which, added to his own, usually results in a net increase in sales.

The top industrial relations man in one of the largest companies in the field study group summed up the influence of job factors in replacing retiring executives. He pointed out that where a man has fulfilled a clearly delineated function within an area of occupational specialization, it is not really difficult when he approaches retirement to find a man with the same specialty who can carry on the assignment. When, however, performance of a job does not rest on prior knowledge, but on the personality, drive, and initiative of the executive involved, the problem posed by the prospective retirement of a successful executive is more significant and difficult for the company to overcome.

3. Job Rotation

In taking the longer view of the impact of retirement on management, companies with a fixed retirement age clearly see the importance of developmental programs in preparing men to take over the jobs of their present superiors at some precise time in the future. There are many inherent difficulties in achieving the objectives of executive succession in the over-all developmental programs of the companies. These broad plans, therefore, encompass certain eventualities. In any group of executives, plans for succession will surely be disrupted by some voluntary retirements, company induced early retirements, resignations for other employment, and death. Retirement at a specific age is the only predictable event for which a company can plan.

Several of the companies see job rotation as a most valuable tool in the development-succession process, for it allows individuals being developed to demonstrate their capabilities in a variety of situations. It also provides, concurrently, the opportunity for management in various areas of a company's operations to gauge the capabilities of younger men. The culmination of the job rotation process occurs when a job vacancy opens at a higher level of the organization, through retirement of older executives. Where rotation and development have been successful, an individual is better prepared to step into several jobs in a company with but a relatively short period of specific job training.

Companies that stress the importance of job rotation as a developmental device draw a distinction between training on the one hand and development on the other. They contend that it is difficult to train a man for a specific managerial job because duties and responsibilities vary greatly from one position to another, and job requirements change over time. If a man is prepared too long in advance for a specific position, it may well be that by the time he gets it, the job has changed. In these companies, it is believed that the broad development of a man is the important thing in equipping him for further executive responsibility.

One company's philosophy on job rotation was expressed as a commentary against on-the-job coaching of a subordinate. It was pointed out that job coaching is unnecessary, since in that company men are trained in the principles of management, and the job rotation program permits them to function in varied work situations. Consequently, when a man takes on a new job, "all he really needs is to find some pencils in the drawer and start to work." Job coaching, which is sometimes referred to as the "buddy system" is, therefore, rejected as being too narrow a training method, especially because it presupposes that the company knows *today* where a man will be needed in the *future*.

The job rotation approach in management development is seen as leading to a continuing supply of managers, which would make the retention of executives beyond the retirement age untenable. Younger managers should "well up" in the organization and be available to step into vacancies, whether caused by retirement, death, or other terminations. An executive with whom this matter was discussed used the analogy of a pipeline in referring to the developmental process in his company. The input is the point of new hire and the outlet of the pipeline is retirement. Keeping the pipeline full is a real job. It requires *forecasting* future manpower needs and keeping *"men in motion,"* so that a large group is available from which to select for any managerial position vacated.

Many executives feel that, ideally, each operating executive should be responsible for the development of his successor. But sometimes this is difficult to achieve, except perhaps at the top level of the organization, because operating executives are problem-oriented, as they should be, whereas the matter of developing men for future responsibility is a continuing long-term process. Moreover, operating departments often take the view that they are bearing the cost of training men for other departments.

4. Pace of Training

In a few cases, company representatives felt that an entirely satisfactory job had been done in gearing the organization for retirements that will occur in the immediate future. This meant that younger men were trained and ready to take over upon the retirement of older men. But in some cases, men had been prepared too long in advance or too rapidly. This overtraining, as it was termed by some executives, was likened to the situation of a boxer who has lost his edge because he was ready for an important match too soon. If an executive is made ready too soon the results can be disastrous for the company, since the overtrained man might become restive and look for employment elsewhere or feel frustrated and become ineffective. Either development could disrupt the planning cycle of succession-retirement.

The action taken by one company to resolve this problem is particularly interesting. Immediate vacancies are created, as warranted, by moving line executives who are approaching retirement into staff assignments. This enables the company to move junior men who are ready for a promotion into the jobs they have been groomed for, while the company can still rely on the availability of their predecessors, should the younger executive need help. In two instances, moves of this kind were made at the vice presidential level, and in both cases freeing the older executives from direct line responsibility was eventually of unforeseen value to the company. Shortly after the shift of one of these men to a staff vice presidency, a problem arose in another operating division because of the poor health of the top line officer. The executive was then moved from the staff assignment to the operating division when the efficiency of the division was threatened. Since he had headed that division some years before, he was taken off his special assignment to run the division, and to develop a back-up man for the operation. Through these and other experiences, the company is convinced that there is considerable value in having a cadre of seasoned top executive officers, free from continuing responsibility, available for emergency or problem assignments.

B. TRANSFER OF RESPONSIBILITY TO SUCCESSORS

The smoothness of succession to executive positions and transfer of attendant responsibilities is viewed in many companies as related to company size. The smaller the company, the greater opportunity a younger man has to observe the work of the man he is expected to succeed. The larger the company, the greater the opportunity for job rotation and the varied preparation it affords.

In one large company which has a program for systematically identifying men with management potential, it was admitted that despite a continuing endeavor to insure smooth transition in effecting executive replacements, transfer of responsibility upon the retirement of a man was frequently jagged. However, it was reported that organizational momentum usually carries a new man through the period of adjustment. The influence of company size was stressed in several of the largest companies in the field study group. It was suggested that because of the stabilizing effect of the organization as a whole, there might be some advantage in throwing an underdeveloped man into a job and letting the organization carry him while he, in effect, trained himself. A possible advantage seen was that new ideas and approaches could emerge when a man without preconceptions about a job takes over.

Because of the diverse patterns followed by the companies in selecting individuals for executive responsibility, there is similar variation in the patterns of transferring responsibility. Among the companies, differences arise because of differences in the types of jobs, and the philosophy of a company about matters of organization and executive development.

1. The "Assistant to" Role

Some companies feel strongly that each manager should have an assistant who in effect is the "heir apparent" to his boss's job. In that position, the man is constantly observing the activities of his boss, and has the opportunity to practice on the job when the boss travels or is on vacation. Upon the retirement of the superior, the assistant is ready to step in and take over. However, other companies react against this method of developing successors. Their reasoning is that if a man is doing only an average job, and his assistant is an especially capable man, the "assistant to" role dulls the energy and stifles the initiative of the subordinate. Opponents of this arrangement also feel that the boss-assistant relationship could lead to conflict, should the views of the two men clash, and such dissension would eventually hinder a smooth transfer of responsibility. However, a topnotch executive frequently carries along an assistant who is nothing more than a good "caddy."

One of the severest indictments of the "assistant to" concept came from one company which for years in the past had believed in and relied heavily on lining up assistants behind responsible executives of the corporation. The company found that this system soon built up much "executive fat" and was imposing considerable cost burdens on the organization. In recent years, overstaffing at the executive levels has been materially reduced, but now the company finds that it has to systematically identify and develop men in preparation for possible promotion. Moreover, the company reports that lines of promotion are no longer as clear as in past years, and transfer of responsibility from one man to another, as retirements occur, has been less smooth with the elimination of "assistant to" positions. Whether or not the price of more or less rough transitions is less than the cost of the past system is a question that is still being evaluated and discussed in the company. The general feeling is, however, that the company is better off by having moved away from the overstaffing that formerly typified the executive organization.

The experience of another company with the use of

assistants has been most satisfactory. Each top executive in the corporation has an assistant who acts as his back-up man. Besides being his boss's deputy, the job of the assistant is clearly defined so that he is directly responsible for a phase of the operation his superior controls. The company finds that this arrangement insures continuity of operations in emergency situations. However, appointment of an assistant is not intended to imply that the assistant will one day succeed to his boss's job. An assistant may be transferred to serve in that role under some other executive, or he may be moved to a managership at a higher level than his present assistantship. The particular promotional move depends, in each case, on the man, the job, and the anticipated needs of the company. This company appraises its system as one which retains smoothness in transfer of executive responsibility, and which has a built-in method of developing men. It provides a degree of variability in the use of assistants, which permits job rotation and discourages the idea that men are simply standing in line waiting for the boss to retire or die.

2. Announcing Replacements

Regardless of the specific method of providing for the transfer of executive responsibility at the time of retirement, there is almost complete agreement among the companies that it is dangerous to announce a successor too long in advance of an actual retirement. The question of what is meant by "too long in advance" did not bring unanimous answers, however. Most generally, executives feel that for operating positions, or positions involving public contact, from three to six months prior to retirement would be the appropriate time to announce, both within and outside the company, the appointment of a man as the successor to a retiring executive.

Most companies reported that they do not actually

designate a successor until almost immediately before a public announcement of the new appointment. This implies that companies generally avoid designating an "heir apparent" well before another man is scheduled to retire. Nevertheless, companies have found that in many instances it is *generally presumed* within a company that a certain man would be promoted to the job of his boss upon the latter's retirement, particularly at the presidential level.

Only a few of the companies studied announce successors well in advance of the time a job will be vacated by the retirement of an incumbent. There were instances in which companies publicly identify some successors as early as two years before the retirement of the executives whose positions they will fill. This is often achieved by promoting a man to a job that historically has led to later promotion to the higher level position. This practice is followed in small plants in small communities, and it is justified on the basis that it is necessary for good public relations to maintain within the community evidence of continuity in plant management. Another reason given for the early announcement of successors is to make possible the transfer of a prospective appointee into a position that permits him to work closely with the man he will be replacing.

3. "Learning By Doing"

Whether as a matter of philosophy as to the best methods of developing men, or because of the practical problems faced and solved in the past, some companies believe that executives should "learn by doing." In these companies, transfer of responsibility and learning the work of an older man tends to take place simultaneously. One illustration of the "learn by doing" philosophy in preparing for the retirement of executives was cited by a company that has a fairly flexible retirement policy, although there is an assumption that retirements will normally occur at age 65. In past years, however, men in this company would "hold on to their jobs until they died with their boots on." Too frequently, this had led to operating crises, for subordinates were not ready to take over when an executive position was vacated.

The management believes that it is impossible to train a man for executive responsibilities, regardless of the management courses or development programs to which he may have been exposed. In recent years, the company has shaped its vacation and leave of absence policies for executives nearing retirement to facilitate application of the "learning by doing" concept. Older men are given fairly long vacation periods or leaves of absence with pay, and during that period, men who had been appointed as assistants do the boss's job. Through these intermittent assignments, the younger man gains direct experience in the job he will eventually handle. Although these men who are selected as future replacements for retiring executives are exposed to various types of developmental activities and work experience, it is the actual practice on the job that the company considers to be the final honing they need.

This company views its policy of flexibility in effecting retirements as an instrument for carrying out its "learning by doing" philosophy. The older man remains available if the younger man fails. He also retains the prestige of his job and the feeling of being able to make a continuing contribution directly or through his successor. Executives in the company believe that this type of arrangement could not be achieved under a mandatory retirement policy, for it would be difficult to justify the required period of time for "taper-off" in an older executive's presence on the job prior to the normal retirement age.

* * *

It has been shown that companies take alternative routes to insure executive succession. But one thing is clear. Company experience in providing for succession upon the retirement of executives demonstrates the importance of viewing executive retirement more broadly than merely termination of the working careers of men.

In many companies in the field study group, there is a high degree of certainty and regularity in the progression of men from job to job, and ultimately up through the executive hierarchy. In these companies there is very little obvious competition for positions, especially at later stages of the promotional cycle. Within certain occupational areas or departments, there is little need to announce in advance who will succeed to a job upon the retirement of a man approaching the mandatory retirement age.

Other companies have no established line of promotion, so that it is important for the chief executive or other executives in the organization to make fairly clear what will happen upon the retirement of men approaching retirement age. The early designation of a successor in these cases is a stabilizing influence, because it minimizes the attempts on the part of a few to maneuver themselves into a position that will become vacant on the retirement of another executive, and for which they feel they are qualified.

Retirement is the final stage of movement of executives through corporate organizations. This movement of men is based on a continuing process of identification, development, preparation for succession, and eventual retirement of executives—all designed to insure the continuity of effective management. Four factors shape the action of companies in transferring responsibility upon retirement at the executive level: public contacts inherent in a position, the scope of administrative responsibility, the degree of specialized occupational information required, and the nature of existing managerial relations. These factors determine the extent of developmental activities and the specific succession patterns established for various executive positions.

CHAPTER VI

Determinants in Retirement- Retention Decisions

THE EXISTENCE OF A FORMAL RETIREMENT POLICY and a pension plan serves to constantly remind executives of the inevitability of retirement. In some companies, executives are contacted to consider plans for their retirement as early as 10 years before their normal retirement date, although one or five years is more common. This is a direct reminder, but more persistent reminders are when other executives reach retirement age and leave the organization, or when executives become involved in planning for successors to their subordinates who are approaching retirement, within the sphere of their own responsibility. In the great majority of cases, retirements occur as a natural event—planned for and accepted—upon the attainment of a prescribed age. Their procedural aspects are determined by company policy and relationships existing among executives in an organization, and usually some form of pageantry surrounds each retirement.

In most cases, retirement is a dramatic moment for both the executive and the company. But this climax in a man's career usually passes quickly and smoothly. In examining this process of separation from employment and into retirement, which is so decisive in the lives of men, there is a tendency to focus on the problem cases rather than on the normal or usual cases. To some extent, this is characteristic of all discussions about retirement. There have been instances, of course, in which executives have resisted retirement, because the individual feels that his abilities and vigor are as great as they ever were. And in some cases where early retirement has been forced by a company, the decision has created a somewhat charged atmosphere at the time of retirement.

The decisions companies make in applying their retirement policies, whether the policy is flexible or mandatory, are discussed in this chapter. Illustrations are given of the circumstances that sometimes compel companies to deviate from their normal retirement practices and decide to delay retirement or temporarily adjust policy, or even change policy. It will be found that deviations from policy generally serve company interest, although frequently both the company and the individual gain. The specific problems that cause companies to effect *early* retirement of executives, and the details of handling such cases, are discussed in the next chapter.

A. INFLUENCE OF RETIREMENT AGE

1. Fixed Retirement Age

Setting retirement at a specific age, as normal company policy, is a most comprehensible approach to retirement. It establishes a uniform and simple rule for determining the retirement date, and obviates the need for special decisions in every case. This precise approach provides an impartial basis for determining retirement of executives. As already shown, 38 of the 46 field study companies have a retirement policy with an established normal retirement age, which is always followed, in some, or is generally followed in others unless unusual circumstances or company interests necessitate deviations.

Although observance of a fixed retirement age alleviates pressures from executives to retain men indefinitely, it also tends to encourage the continued employment of executives who are no longer measuring up to their responsibilities. For only in extreme and clearly identifiable cases of breakdown in performance do companies effect retirements before a specified age, and companies frequently reported that in some such situations it is possible to find ways of using an older man even though it may be in an area of responsibility other than the one he occupied earlier in his career. The more general tendency is to carry men through to the normal or mandatory retirement age.

Companies in the field study group find it difficult to determine whether or not an executive's performance in his job has lagged. For example, if an executive is developing a potential successor by coaching him on the job, there comes a time when he would gradually transfer some direct responsibilities to him. But as further responsibilities are shifted, it may become difficult to appraise whether the extent of work load transferred to a subordinate is in the interest of developing him, or is a sign that his superior has abandoned his normal responsibilities.

Despite the difficulty of identifying poor executive performance, many of the companies studied recognize the problem, yet are carrying executives along to the specified retirement age. This matter plagues both large and small companies. In large organizations, the poor performer is hidden, and it is difficult to isolate him. In the small organization, the executive group tends to be closely knit as a working and social group, and, where poor performance is recognized, it is difficult to make the decision to force early retirement on a man who is a colleague and friend. This same problem often prevails at the plant level of larger companies, where a small executive group has the same sort of close work and social contacts as is so frequently the case in smaller companies.

One of the prime reasons cited for not forcing an ineffective executive into early retirement is that such action is viewed as damaging to a man's dignity. Much stress was laid on this point in interviews with company executives. It is also the reason why some companies eschew flexible retirement approaches. In the absence of objective measures of executive effectiveness, companies are generally disposed to adhere to the normal retirement date, regardless of individual performance. This desire to preserve individual dignity and avoid the personal hurt, through the impartial use of a chronological age for retirement, has caused many companies to be more or less rigid in applying a formal retirement age. The companies feel, however, that a more logical approach to retirement would be one that would permit the weeding out of deadwood and the retention of men who remain capable.

2. Flexible Retirement Age

In only eight of the field study companies is retirement of executives handled with some degree of flexibility. Most retirements have occurred, however, at the age established by the pension plan as a basis for computing pension credits. Thus, even in companies with relatively flexible retirement policy, there tends to be a fairly systematic age pattern for retirement, although there have been variations based on decisions about an individual's ability to continue to work.

It is interesting to find that even companies in this group feel that they have not done as effective a job as needed in weeding out executive deadwood. By their own reasoning, these companies actually do not take an entirely flexible approach, for flexibility should mean retiring men before, as well as after, the normal retirement age. Apparently, the previously cited diffidence of management to terminate executives on the basis of performance, regardless of age, creates a pressure in all companies, regardless of policy, to recognize a normal retirement date and stick to it.

3. Illustrations of Retirement Practices

Throughout the study, specific problem situations and historic precedents emerged as far more compelling in determining company retirement practices than philosophical beliefs in either a fixed or a flexible retirement age. Whether companies currently follow a fixed or a flexible retirement policy, the particular policy has been shaped by developments and experience within the individual company. To illustrate the considerations that bring about adjustments and changes in policy, the experience of six companies is reviewed below. These are cases in which retirement practices are unique, or the companies have recently modified or see a need to modify their customary retirement policy. In each case the retirement approach is related to the necessities of over-all staffing.

Case 1: Reappraising Flexible Retirement. This is the case of a company that has followed a policy of extreme flexibility in effecting retirements, but in which current pressures by younger men are forcing a reassessment and systematization of retirement policy. The company was founded early in 1930 and has expanded greatly, especially during the war years. The founding fathers are still on the scene and are influential in determining the current success of the business. Because of its tie to the past, the company never established a mandatory retirement age, as many other companies did. It now follows a normal retirement age of 65, but there is considerable flexibility in retaining men above that age.

The first retirement plan was introduced primarily for hourly-paid employees, and initially the retirement age was established at 65. Because of pressures on the part of older employees in the unionized group, the company began to permit individuals to remain through to their 68th year at their own option. This tended to parallel the practice at the executive level, where men who had been associated with the company from its beginnings, including the founder of the company, may continue in employment beyond 65, and some for as long as they choose.

Certain executives within the company feel that such an approach gives a high degree of continuity to the management concepts on which the organization was founded and has been based over the years. Coupled with this idea is the belief among executives that it is impossible to determine retirement age on the basis of chronological factors alone. Individual selection for retirement is therefore considered to be the only satisfactory basis for determining actual retirement dates.

Today, younger executives question this approach, but they also see advantages in the continued employment of several valuable older men. Thus, this company's retirement approach is in flux. The early pattern set by retaining production workers beyond normal retirement age, which coincides with the desires of most of the older executives, has progressively developed an extremely high degree of flexibility in handling retirement. Apart from assessing whether the company's retirement plan should be entirely rigid or entirely flexible, executives are trying to find the best ways of effecting retirements to serve the best interest of the company, in terms of attracting and holding younger executives.

Case 2: Tapering Off Employment. This rather small company has a most ingenious plan for bringing working careers with the company to a conclusion, through a taper-off arrangement. The attractiveness of the plan lies in its apparent flexibility and equity. However, it is the specific circumstances within the company which led to the development of the plan and which permit it to work. The plan was developed some 10 years ago, for two reasons. First, the company was encumbered at that time with many men who had remained at work beyond their normal retirement age and who were receiving both salary and pension. Given the combination of incomes, it became practically impossible to force a man into retirement, regardless of his age or ability. Second, for a variety of reasons many individuals in the company were employed late in life—especially in plant jobs. Thus, their retirement benefit at age 65 was not as high a proportion of final earnings as the company felt it should be, and continued employment became a means of supplementing retirement income.

Today, under the company's present plan, individual selection of retirement age and income reduction are tied together. Each individual, regardless of whether he works in the plant or headquarters office, chooses whether or not he will stay on in employment after reaching the normal retirement age of 65. In order to remain beyond that age, however, the man *must* select the number of years after age 65 for which he wishes to continue to work. His election is then approved by the executive committee of the board of directors, and the age coinciding with the extended period of employment he selects, becomes his compulsory retirement age. However, for each year after 65 that the man works, his work period is reduced by one month.

In a man's 66th year, he is compensated for 11 months —the period he is at work, plus paid vacation—and has to take a leave of absence without pay of one month, but during such leaves he is not eligible for pension. In his 67th year, he is compensated for 10 months and has a two months' leave of absence. The concept behind this reduction in work period is that a man would soon "wean himself away from employment" by spending more time away from the job than on the job. Theoretically, if a man stayed to his 77th year, he would then be compensated for only one month in the year and would be away for 11 months without pay or pension.

The company feels its plan to be as sound a retirement method as can be conceived, for it provides a method of easing men into retirement under an arrangement where both the company and individual adjust slowly to the impact of retirement. It is believed also that the plan avoids conflicts by eventually forcing complete retirement through the income reduction feature of the taper-off formula. Furthermore, the plan allows a man who is retained beyond the normal retirement age to continue to build up pension credits, rather than receive a pension while in employment.

The taper-off formula is designed to make it uneconomical for a man of 68 years of age to continue in employment. By that time, his retirement income becomes attractive when he compares his reduced salary with what he could receive through the pension plan and social security, if he were not working. It was most interesting to find that since the inception of the plan no retiring executive had postponed retirement under these taper-off provisions even though the company is small. At the time of the field visit, however, one man in a high executive position had just selected an option which would permit him to stay on in employment beyond age 65. While the company feels that this plan is particularly valuable, it is difficult to visualize its adaptability in a larger company where arranging for staff coverage of jobs when men are on paid leave of absence could be a problem.

Case 3: Allowing for Selective Retention. In this case, the retirement plan is essentially mandatory but borrows some features of flexible plans. The company established a policy early in 1958, providing for normal retirement at age 65, with retirement mandatory at 68. Retention up to age 68 is subject to approval in a review made at age 65. Previous to this arrangement, age 65 was the normal retirement age, but a considerable number of executives were retained beyond that age. However, retention in those years was not based on any established criteria. The new approach provides a convenient administrative procedure whereby individuals can be screened at the normal retirement age and retained in employment only if still qualified to continue in their positions, or are forced into retirement if they are no longer efficient. At the same time, the mandatory feature establishes a terminal age for employment.

The company sees two long-range advantages in its plan. First, it identifies employees who continue to be an asset to the organization as well as those who, for health or other reasons, are no longer contributing to the corporation. Second, the opportunity for selective retention after age 65, and not beyond age 68, results in savings in pension costs. When a man works three or more years after age 65, pension benefits are not paid. Since life span remains relatively constant after age 65, over-all costs are reduced and monies already accumulated are accruing interest for the three-year period during which there is no pay-out.

The company's retirement practice has a further immediate advantage. Developments within the company over the last several years have necessitated the retention of certain men in senior executive positions. Vacancies have occurred in the management organization through expansion, rapid executive turnover, and retirement. This plan has provided a limited yet systematic means of retaining needed people, without inviting demands by all employees for a continuation of their employment.

Case 4: Multiple Practices Within a Company. In another company, differing retirement policies have come into existence in the several divisions of the company. The president observed that these differences have arisen because of his own uncertainty about which is the soundest approach to executive retirement. He stated that the difference in policies in effect in the divisions are a reflection of the evolution of his own views over time about retirement and in relationship to differing conditions. In one division, there is an entirely flexible approach to the handling of retirements, while in another division, the practice is to retire men arbitrarily at age 65.

The company's multiple practices were justified on the basis that each division views itself as an autonomous operating unit, in which practices should be more closely related to those in the industry in which the division is active, than to an over-all company policy. This rationalization may permit alternative policies to exist side by side, but this does not mean that the headquarters executive staff is entirely satisfied with the current varied policy approach. While men at the top presented many interesting ideas on retirement policy, there was a general disposition within the company to lean toward a more systematic retirement policy to facilitate executive staffing, even though there were advocates of entirely flexible retirement practices.

Case 5: Policy in Transition. In this company, there has always been a flexible approach to retirement, especially because of the influence of its founders, who have passed from the corporate scene only recently. At the time of the field study, no interest was found at top levels within the company to modify the retirement policy. However, there is a growing recognition and use of age 65 as the retirement age for executives. This developing practice stems from corporate staffing problems.

Each of the last several presidents were over age 60 when they took office. Many of the executives feel that this is too advanced an age at which to start running the company, for more aggressive energetic leadership is required, and a man must have enough time to make his mark on the company. Thus, methods of enabling chief executives to emerge somewhat earlier in their working careers are being sought, in order to provide longer periods of continuity in top management. It is believed in the company that the recognition of age 65 as the retirement age will be helpful to the making of staffing decisions earlier in the working life of executives. Not only will succession be determined earlier, therefore, but it will also be smoother and more systematic in the future.

Case 6: Revolutionizing Retirement Policy. This is the case of a company that changed its retirement policy from flexible to mandatory during the course of this study. The company had always taken an informal approach to retirement, although with the adoption of a pension plan it was assumed that retirements would occur at the age the plan specifies as the normal retirement age. However, the company continued to allow individuals to remain in employment after that age, especially within the executive organization. About 10 years ago, a fairly young man became president, and he found around him an older and highly inbred executive group. In appraising the future, the president felt it important to weed out older men and to bring into the executive group "new, energetic, and imaginative executives." He felt that men of this caliber were available within the company, but their promotion was blocked by older men.

After struggling with this problem of staffing, the president examined company approaches to retirement, and decided that a rigidly applied mandatory retirement age would be helpful, at least at this point in the company's development. But the president delayed recommending a change in policy to the board for two reasons. First, the president wanted to gain acceptance for a mandatory age among his staff. Second, there were anticipated changes on the board, because of age, which had to occur before the proposed policy on retirement would be looked upon with favor. Older men on the board, some of them substantial stockholders, who had been employees and were still influential in the company, would have opposed the mandatory retirement age, even though they were no longer affected as employees. Within the last year, however, the president introduced such a policy and it was approved.

In examining his problem, this executive was impressed, as were others, with the continuing control that could be exerted over a company by only a few men. For example, if a president takes over his position at age 50 and continues in the job to 70 years of age, he would have been president for 20 years. A previous president might have been in office for 25 years, having retired at the age of 75. In such a situation, which could have been common to many companies in the past, only two men would have been responsible for the guidance of the company for almost half a century. Similar periods of individual control would be possible with respect to other positions of high responsibility in a company.

In the company in question, the president feels that with the change in policy many of the past problems of attracting and retaining younger men and getting new blood into the executive organization can be overcome. Moreover, the company is provided with an arbitrary formula for determining when the president himself must retire, and this is seen as an important control.

4. Alternative Guides Suggested by Executives

To achieve variability in retirement, without adverse effects on executive motivation and morale, requires more incisive guides for differentiating among individuals on the basis of their abilities than are available to management. Here, perhaps, is the greatest challenge to the art and science of management for the next decade.

a. Differentiating Between Mental and Physical Aging: One method of determining a man's ability to continue to work effectively later in life was mentioned by a few executives in the course of this study. It is the Halstead Battery for Differential Aging,[12] which attempts to go far beyond the practice of using evaluations of job performance and medical reports as an aid in reaching decisions about retention or retirement of executives. This battery is a series of tests, including a neurological examination of the structure of the eye, and a series of standardized tests of fact grasping, fact reten-

[12] This discussion of the Halstead Battery is based on an interview with, and written material provided by, Dr. W. C. Halstead, head of the Department of Medical Psychology at the University of Chicago.

tion, decision making, and power drive. On the results, certain conclusions about relative aging are based. The battery of tests was developed through research connected with the psychological elements of the executive health program sponsored by the University of Chicago.

Halstead believes that the examination and tests provide a basis for differentiating between executive abilities according to biological factors, rather than chronological age. While Halstead does not hold that his battery should be used to govern the retirement-retention decision, an experimental three-company sample has shown that the battery results correlate highly with ratings of performance by chief executives. Even on this limited evidence, some executives showed interest in the Halstead battery or the development of something like it, as a tool to assist management in making sharp and realistic decisions about retirement.

b. Making Judgments on Performance: While methods such as the Halstead battery take an almost clinical approach in determining differences between biological and chronological age, more pragmatic approaches can be adopted. The simplest and most direct is for a responsible executive to judge the ability of a man to continue in employment. Decisions made on this basis are felt by many executives interviewed to be no different from the decisions which every executive has to make about salary and promotion throughout a subordinate's career.

Others, however, consider the retirement determination a singularly important one, and that several judgments should be obtained in the process. They see value, therefore, in establishing committees to consider the retention or retirement of men. In a few companies this approach had been thought through and discussed among the executives, and they envision an arrangement whereby such committees would consist of officers and board members, who would have available to them medical counsel about men being considered for retention or retirement. An arrangement of this kind would parallel the panels established under the armed services review board system, as discussed in a later chapter.

c. Setting Minimum Job Tenure: A most interesting approach to the problem of determining who should be retired and who should be retained is based on an entirely different view of the retirement problem by a few executives. It establishes the proposition that retirement should not be controlled by the age of a man, but by the needs of the company and the demands of a job. The standard for job tenure would be that, if a particular job required a period of 10 years for a man to make the contribution expected of him, this period of time would determine his duration of service, not his retirement age. This "minimum service" standard for a job would take precedence over a normal retirement age. Thus, if a man at age 60 moved into a job with a seven years' service requirement, in a company with a normal retirement age of 65, the man would remain in employment through to his 67th year. There are obvious difficulties in such an approach, but the basic principle might have interesting application to the top two or three jobs in a corporation, or perhaps for members of a board of directors.

B. RETENTION ARRANGEMENTS

In preceding discussions references have been made to the retention of executive skills as an important factor in staffing the organization and in handling the retirement of executives. Retention arrangements take a variety of forms, but all are designed to meet the needs of the company in overcoming immediately pressing problems or shortages of manpower. The three general methods by which the companies retain executives after men have reached a normal or mandatory retirement age are:

1. Retention in regular employment, as an exception to normal retirement policy.

2. Retention after retirement as a consultant—the far more frequent practice among the companies.

3. Retention after termination as employee or officer, by election to the board of directors, or appointment to special committees of the board.

1. Retaining Executives as Employees

Retaining a man in employment after he has reached the normal retirement age appears especially attractive when the individual has been singularly successful in his activities and when it is unlikely that he can be replaced easily. It was found that companies often retain highly successful managers, scientists or engineers who have made a unique contribution to their company's success.

While all of the field study companies do not allow retention of men after they have reached the normal or mandatory retirement age, a group of 12 of the 46 provide as a matter of policy that men may be retained when it is in the best interests of the company to do so. Seventeen of the companies had in employment at the time of the field study at least one executive who had passed the normal retirement age.

In most cases, retention in employment is regarded as an exception to retirement policy and must be approved by the board of directors—for all employees in some companies, for only top executive officers in others, or for employees in special assignments or special problem situations. Generally, these approvals are valid for only a specified period of time. Among the companies, two general procedures are followed in obtaining approval for retaining an executive, and under each the individual's health is considered, but this factor is not necessarily controlling:

1. A man's immediate superior reports the need to retain the man in his job, to his own superior, who in turn makes a recommendation to the president. The president or the executive committee then recommends an action to the board of directors, or a committee of the board, which approves or disapproves the extension of employment beyond retirement age. This is the majority practice.

2. The immediate superior recommends, either to the executive vice president of the company or to the president, that the man be continued in employment, and the appropriate officer may approve or disapprove the recommendation. This practice is followed in only three of the field study companies.

The retention of executives in companies with a mandatory retirement age is generally for a definite period, with a renewal of the period possible. Generally the companies permit an extension for one-year periods, although only three-month periods are allowed in two of the companies. These extensions are frequently designed to permit an executive to complete an assignment or task on which he is working immediately prior to his retirement date. It is viewed as impractical in many companies to force a man into retirement on a given day if a few more weeks or months might permit him to conclude an assignment.

Two other practices should be noted, although they are not considered an extension of employment. In some companies, men reaching the normal retirement age are continued in employment up to a certain date, related generally to a board of directors' meeting. A man who is an officer and director of the company is required to tender his resignation to the board. His resignation is not effective until the next annual board meeting following his normal retirement date, and in some cases this could extend employment almost a year after retirement age is reached. Similarly, the bonus distribution plan in a few companies provides for the distribution to be made on a certain date following the close of the company's fiscal year, or at the end of the calendar year. As a matter of practice, men reaching retirement within the calendar year prior to the date of bonus distribution are continued until bonus time, so that they may participate in the plan during their last year of employment. Because these practices are matters of administrative form or convenience for the retiree and not devices to defer retirement, they are not considered below in the tally of companies permitting retention in employment beyond retirement age.

a. Justification of Requests for Retention: The common justification for retaining a man in employment after he has reached the normal retirement age is that he will make a continued contribution to the company. In almost all of the companies permitting it, retention in employment must have some apparent rational basis. This is seen by the companies as the method by which requests for a continuation of employment can be controlled.

The practice in one company is typical. It establishes three conditions which must be met if an employee is to be retained in employment. First, the man must be earning no more than a specified salary. Second, the superior must show that no replacement is available. Third, the executive recommending retention must cite an extreme emergency which warrants continuation of employment, or the man must be on an assignment that only he can fulfill and which cannot be completed before his normal retirement date. A fourth condition, formalized in policy in only one company, is that the man must be "in a unique position to make a contribution to the business."

In at least five of the companies with a policy permitting retention of executives beyond the normal retirement age, recommendations for retention of executives are frowned on, because they imply a breakdown in the management development program, or in executive planning. In one of these companies, any executive requesting permission to retain a man in employment is considered to be offering prima facie evidence of his own shortcomings in not having anticipated the crisis which his request for retention implies. In each of the other four companies, retention is considered only when an emergency makes it absolutely necessary.

b. Conditions Under Which Retention Is Allowed: Companies which retain executives in employment after they have reached the normal retirement age are difficult to typify. Men are retained under conditions and in response to circumstances which vary widely. Usually, the retention of a man is for practical reasons, and the fact that a company may have a fixed retirement age is not allowed to stand in the way of company interests. One illustration is the retention of older engineers and scientists by many companies in the field study group. Retaining these men relieves the pressure of shortages of skilled men, and the older men are generally found to be well able to continue to contribute to the manufacturing process or to research and development activities. Only a relatively small number of men are retained by companies because they have a significant ownership interest in the business. Evidently this factor is far less prevailing today than was the case in many of these companies some years ago.

In some companies, it is clear that the nature of certain positions demands a degree of continuity in contacts outside the company. Examples of this are men in sales positions or plant managers who have a public relations value in their local communities. Other men are valuable because of their relationships with governmental agencies or their legislative contacts. Normal training, developmental and succession patterns cannot be easily geared to the replacing of men who have such contacts. Similarly, in banking and insurance companies, men with contacts or board memberships in other concerns are of special value to a company, and arrangements for retirement are often worked out individually in order to permit retention in the interests of the employee and the company.

In a few manufacturing companies, men have been retained in special assignments in overseas operations. In each case, the situation is similar, in that the company is drawing on the services of men who are familiar with its operations, who are uniquely qualified to assist in the establishment of plants overseas, and whose capacities have not been dulled by age.

These observations suggest that executive retention patterns are a function of interrelated factors pertaining to the business as well as to the individual's qualifications. Philosophy about adhering to retirement age policy does not always outweigh the practicality of retaining a man who is needed.

Despite what is practical, however, a caveat offered by the president of one company which retains a large number of individuals beyond the normal retirement age is in order. He indicated that, while the ability to retain men puts the company in a particularly favorable position with respect to the peculiar or unusual skills of individual executives, the company must still recognize the necessity of terminating individuals who are no longer able to do their jobs effectively. His dilemma, echoed in many companies, is how to terminate a man once he has been retained. It is this fear of indefinite retention that has caused companies to adopt the practice of renewing extensions beyond the normal retirement age annually. Each request for renewal of a retirement extension provides an opportunity to reconsider and possibly reject the request if conditions have changed.

2. Retaining Retired Executives as Consultants

Twenty of the 46 field study companies reported that they permit executives to be retained as consultants after retirement. The consultant relationship subsequent to retirement often is only another device for keeping executive skills available to a company. Consultant arrangements vary in purpose, in extent of use within companies, and in duration. Companies look favorably upon such arrangements because they permit management to draw on the special talents of experienced executives, but without retaining them in employment. Thus, a company can avoid setting precedents which may lead to requests from other executives to extend their active service.

While the consulting arrangement keeps an executive available to the company, his status as a retiree, instead of an employee, makes him generally ineligible for participation in various fringe benefits, including vacations, and in group benefit plans. While these are not substantial cost items, it is reported that they can multiply to significant proportions, and entail cumulative administrative details.

In some instances the consulting arrangements made with retired executives are of indefinite duration, while in others they are for specific periods, depending on the reason for retaining the individual. Some arrangements are made with retirees to maintain a tie-in with their former company, although they are not given precise assignments. Time spent at work as a consultant varies directly with the consulting assignment. Men may be at work full time, half time, or they may merely be "on call."

The approvals necessary for entering into a consulting arrangement with a retired executive vary considerably among the companies. In some, it is possible for an officer of the company or a high-level operating executive to approve the arrangement. In others, approval must be given by the board of directors; such approval may be simply a matter of form in some companies, or rather difficult to obtain in others. In several companies a retirement committee, referred to in some instances as an employee welfare committee, approves each such arrangement. Such committees are often committees of the board of directors.

The following review of the purposes served through consulting relationships between a company and a retired executive indicates the range of problems that lead to such arrangements. The nature of these problems determines the extent to which the retired executives are used, and for how long a period.

a. Work on Specialized Assignments: The most common consulting arrangement is for a retired executive to provide service or guidance to the company in an area in which he has specialized knowledge. Illustrations of this were men who are specialists in product design, tax law, engineering, international operations, geological and exploratory activities, agricultural field maintenance, and special phases of the accounting or financial fields.

In several companies in the field study group, retired

men have been retained to provide services on a particularly knotty tax problem. One case serves to illustrate the need to recall an executive as a consultant for a specialized assignment. In this company the corporate tax return for a previous year was challenged, and the executive who had worked out the details of the treatment of the particular tax matter questioned had retired. Having been a specialist on income tax problems, he was brought back into employment as a consultant for the period that the problem was being worked out with the tax authorities.

b. Specific Advisory Role: One of the most repeated reasons given by companies for retaining retired executives is to draw on their past experience by engaging them as advisors to operating management. The rationale is that a man who has spent many years in employment in a company knows the company, its activities, and its industry, and since he is removed from day-to-day administrative burdens, he is in an excellent position to give advice on current company problems. Such guidance and counsel, based on experience, is particularly valuable where the executive staff is made up largely of relatively young men.

In some cases, retired executives are retained to provide guidance and direction to a young successor who had not gained enough experience on the job prior to the older man's retirement, or to a young executive who, through turnover in the executive ranks, had moved up to a job faster than was planned. A development of this sort occurred when, in one company, the successor to a retired executive died shortly after taking over his new position. The retired executive was recalled to provide guidance and to help in the development of a younger man who was appointed to the vacant post.

An interesting case brings into perspective a problem that could arise when a retired executive is retained to give guidance to a younger man. In interviews throughout one company, members of the executive organization reported that a retired executive working as a consultant was providing an important and valuable service to the company. His case was cited as a justification of the company's realistic approach in retaining able men, especially as the consultant was seen as being of special help to the operating executive who had succeeded him when he retired. However, the present operating executive viewed the consultant as a continuing problem. He claimed that the older man tended to get involved in the operating aspects of the job, for those were the activities the older man knew well. Because the consultant found it difficult to separate himself from the job, problems were created for the younger man, especially as the staff continued to look to the consultant for leadership rather than to the younger executive who was then responsible. The problem was solved, in part, by moving the consultant's office away from the immediate vicinity of the department which he formerly headed.

In another company, a retiring executive retained as a consultant recognized for himself the possibility of causing operating problems for his replacement. Upon his retirement, therefore, he relinquished his former office. He felt that his action was symbolic of his retirement and would underscore that fact to men who formerly reported to him.

c. General Consulting Relationships: In a number of cases, executives retained as consultants after retirement are not assigned any specific tasks. Commonly, such undefined consulting arrangements have the objective of providing a retiree with additional retirement income, while the individual remains "on call," should the company need his services. This is most often true in the case of company officers. In some situations, individuals have been retired shortly after the installation or liberalization of a pension plan, and the company considers their accrued pension at the time of retirement as hardly adequate. To offset such deficiencies, companies retain men under general consulting arrangements, and make out-of-pocket payments to supplement their retirement income.

These supplements are regarded as a recognition of length of service which has not been commensurately taken into account by the pension plan. Nevertheless, the companies further justify the additional payments by a proviso that men receiving such emoluments shall hold themselves available for consulting purposes if the company desires. The need for consulting arrangements of this type diminishes, of course, with the passage of time. In a rather large company, which in the past had this arrangement with numerous retired executives, the number has been dropping steadily —with only seven men still so retained at the time of the field study.

Many of the mail survey companies provided information on the amount of time executives retained as consultants actually spend at work. Of the 228 companies, 105 reported such data for only 204 retirees, as follows:

Service as a Consultant (as a Percent of Normal Full-Time Work)	Number of Executives
Less than one-fourth	146
About one-third	19
About one-half	14
About two-thirds	7
About three-fourths	18
Total	204

It is significant that so large a proportion of the consultants provide less than a quarter of their time in service to their former companies. This appears to substantiate the generally minor role attributed to the retiree-consultant in the comments of executives in both the mail survey and field study companies.

The amount and duration of payments made under such arrangements naturally vary among companies. In range, they may be a minimum of $6,000 per year and may reach up to 50 percent of what a man earned in salary at the time of his retirement. While consultant status is usually established on a year-to-year basis, requiring repeated approvals, it is generally continued for from three to five years, based "on the degree to which the executive consultant does not get into the hair of the active corporate management." It was observed by some interviewees that whenever a consultant tries to act like one, his arrangement is not renewed.

In one company's experience, a retired executive was retained in employment after reaching normal retirement age in order to improve what otherwise would have been a minimal retirement benefit. Subsequently, the company began to enforce its normal retirement age, and the man was separated from employment but retained as a consultant. He carefully observes the 9:00 to 5:00 five-day workweek, and continues to report all absences, and the reasons for them. Although there is a common understanding that this man provides no service for the company that could not be provided by others, the management feels that having embarked on an arrangement with him, the company cannot renege on it. The regular attendance of the retiree has become an annoying reminder of special arrangements made in the past when the normal retirement age was not observed.

Two interesting sidelights were disclosed during discussions in the field study companies which are opposed to the retention of individuals, on any basis, after they have reached the mandatory retirement age. In one case, men have been retained as consultants because of their special knowledge of given problems, but through a third party, so that the company is not directly involved in making a consulting arrangement with the man. In another company, it was found that retired engineers and scientists were being retained at plant locations, even though company policy prohibits their retention as employees or consultants. The method of doing this is to retain the men as "independent contractors." Although this circumvention of policy amounts to legal fiction, it permits plant management to skirt company policy and retain a retired man when it is essential to do so.

d. Arrangements to Protect Competitive Position: Several companies have been faced with a competitive problem because retiring executives had sought and obtained positions in other companies operating in the same product and market area, which put these men in competition with the company from which they had retired. A company officer offered an illustration of this situation in his company, where a man from an important division producing a highly competitive product retired and was offered a position in a competing firm. It was apparent that unless some arrangement was made *to use* the man's services *and compensate* him, he would be hired by the competitor to the detriment of his former company's interests. A consulting arrangement was therefore made with the retired executive which was more attractive for him than employment elsewhere, because it permitted him to arrange his activities to suit himself, whereas the competitor had wanted his services on a full-time basis.

The matter of protecting a company's competitive position is considered by management to be an entirely appropriate basis for entering into financial agreements with certain retiring executives. Under such circumstances, consulting arrangements generally appeal to men whose need is to remain active rather than to simply gain additional income.

While retention as a consultant is the common arrangement to keep retired executives from joining a competitive organization, various other methods are followed. Some companies established deferred compensation plans which are designed to forestall any moves on the part of retired executives to seek or accept employment with a competitor. Under such plans, company payments are contingent on a man remaining in a retired role or clearing any prospective employment with his former company.

Many pension plans have similar features, which are referred to as "bad boy clauses." These clauses restrict postretirement assignments that officers of a company may engage in, and give a company the right to cease paying a pension if it finds that employment after retirement is in conflict with the best interests of the company.

A few companies have provided extra amounts in the form of a supplement to a pension, to keep men from competitive employment. In one company, retired executives receive a paid-up life insurance policy equalling one-half of annual salary at retirement. Retired men see this as a valuable benefit; but the policy could be canceled should an executive take employment with a competitor.

A substantial minority of the companies studied had not faced problems in this area. The experience of one of these companies has been that retirees who worked elsewhere frequently directed business to their former company; the management has never thought, therefore, of restricting the executives from working after retirement.

It was anticipated in this study that many companies would be found to have employment contracts with their executives. In only a very few cases, however, were there employment contracts binding a company to guarantee job tenure of specific duration, including post-retirement consultation. Such contracts as were found covered men through to their normal retirement date, and then into a period of consultancy after retirement. They generally applied to men who were recruited from outside the company to fill executive openings which otherwise would have been difficult to fill. The men who took such jobs demanded some guarantee of job security and retirement income, to offset the loss of accrued benefits from their former companies.

C. RETIREMENT AT THE BOARD LEVEL

The fact that a man is an officer and director in a company adds another dimension to the retirement issue. If a man who is a company officer is required to retire at a specified age, does he also retire from his directorship at the same time? This question stimulated much discussion by executives and board members who were interviewed in the course of this study.

It is fairly generally held among companies that the qualifications which make a man a satisfactory officer of a company are not necessarily the same as those which determine whether an individual would be a satisfactory board member over the long term. Companies usually take a different approach in the handling of retirement for inside directors as compared with outside directors. Alternatively, where a company follows a practice of using an inside board exclusively, there is generally an established policy that when a man retires as an employee, he retires from the board at the same age.

A few companies follow a clear practice of retaining men who have reached the officer level of the company by providing for their promotion to the board of directors upon reaching the company's normal retirement age. Additionally, in at least four of the companies there appeared to be a fairly clear path from the presidency to chairmanship of the board. In no case, however, was this progression provided for by policy. In several cases, a retiring president is assured of board membership after retirement but not the chairmanship.

The justification for retaining an executive on the board after retirement is that by this means the advice and counsel of an officer remain available to the company. Generally, such men have been in a position of guiding the company over a long number of years, and they can continue to be valuable in the future because of their intimate knowledge of the company and its industry. The difference in the burden involved in a day-to-day administrative job, as against the policy-making, goal-setting role of a board member makes possible a continued contribution.

1. Retirement of Officer-Board Members

Normally, when an officer-director retires as an officer, his retirement from the board occurs at the same time. The policies of the majority of the companies differ only with respect to the specific age at which retirement occurs. The following tabulation gives the normal retirement age for board members in 21 field study companies providing such information. It permits comparison of the retirement age for officer-directors with the retirement age for men who are outside board members. The specific retirement ages are shown in the order of their frequency among the companies:

Retirement Age For—		Number of Companies
Officer-Directors	Outside Directors	
*IR	*IR	6
65	*IR	4
65	70	3
68	72	2
75	75	2
65	68	1
65	72	1
68	70	1
70	70	1

Total companies 21

* IR—Indefinite retention.

In a majority of cases, outside directors may remain on the board well beyond the retirement age established for officer-directors. Three companies follow a normal retirement age of 65 for all executives including officers, but permit an officer who is also a director to remain on the board through to age 68. In the six companies which permit indefinite retention on the board, for both officer-directors and outside directors, a man generally retires as an officer at the normal retirement age established by the company. However, three of these companies have informal or general agreements with officer-directors that they will retire from board membership at ages 72, 75, or 78, respectively, but as a matter of policy they allow indefinite retention of outside board members.

Among the field study companies, there has been a growing recognition of the need for a retirement age for board members, and there is general agreement that as older men retire from their board positions, a more systematic approach will have to be taken to their retirement. This has led to the establishment of both formal and informal retirement age policies for board members in many companies, incorporating what are termed "grandfather clauses," which permit men who are presently active to be retained indefinitely. These special clauses make it difficult to categorize many of the company policies precisely.

Several of the companies reported that problems are beginning to develop because of the advanced age of board members. Generally, the older members represent outside interests and have been associated with the company over the years. In one company, however, its former officers who are now of advanced age have remained on the board. As reported by the president of this company, a great wave of young men moved into the company in the 1920's. These men assumed responsible positions and were not followed by other new entrants during the 30's and early 40's, for very few men were hired during the depression and war years. This accounts not only for the high proportion of older employees within the company and for the general pattern of flexible retirement, but also for the retention of older men as board members. The company now requires a chairman of the board to relinquish his responsibilities upon reaching his 75th year. There has been no formalization of a retirement age policy for board members in general, however, although the president feels that at some point a specific age will probably be required, whether it be 70, 72, or 75.

In one company where normal retirement for executives is at age 65, and retirement for board members is informally set at 72, officer-directors have not remained on the board after their retirement as officers. In the case of a past president, a seven-year consulting arrangement was made prior to his recent retirement, whereby he will remain active, both as a member of the board and as a consultant to the operating president of the company for a specified period of years. Normally, however, a retiring president assumes the responsibilities of chairman of the board or chairman of the executive committee, whichever position is open. Thus, the pattern here is for the retiring president to move to a higher position that is disassociated from the day-to-day administrative role he had played before retirement.

2. Differences in Retirement Ages

A common opinion among the executives interviewed was that there is nothing wrong with or inconsistent about a difference in retirement age for outside directors in comparison to inside directors. The value of an officer-director is as a representative of the management of the company. But upon retirement it is believed that an officer loses touch with the activities within the company rather quickly. By the end of his second year of retirement there may be serious question as to his familiarity with the current internal problems of the company. Believing this to be the case, it is far more sensible to terminate a man as a director and permit a new man who is in close touch with internal management to take his post.

The outside member on the other hand is brought to the board for a different set of reasons than an inside member. His job is (1) to represent outside interests, perhaps a majority stockholder group, (2) to bring to his position special experience or contacts, and, (3) to examine and analyze company problems in a broad frame of reference. The outside board member is there to consider and provide judgment on matters of policy. As stated by one executive, "At the board level you are concerned with wisdom and not energy." In many cases, the outside board member is viewed as a man with valuable contacts which are important to the company. In some cases he is seen as a watchdog. These are all characteristics and abilities which do not necessarily diminish with age.

3. Changed Approaches

Several companies reported that they have made recent changes in their methods for handling the retirement of board members. Two of the companies which follow a policy of mandatory retirement at age 65 now permit an inside board member to remain on the board through to his 68th year. Both companies made this change approximately three years ago—one as a matter of formal policy, the other under an informal agreement among the board members. The prime value seen by the companies in this arrangement is that it gives the director a three-year period in which to stimulate action at the board level in areas where he might not have had the time to work while still an officer.

Another company had never had a mandatory retirement age for outside board members until four years ago, when it established one at age 68. Two other companies established, approximately three years ago, a mandatory retirement age of 72 for outside board members. In several other cases, however, informal changes have been made with respect to a terminal age for board membership. Generally it has been difficult to introduce retirement ages for board members because of the average age of the present board members. The older the members, the more resistance there is to a fixed retirement age. This explains the many "grandfather clauses." It also explains the expediency of drawing up informal agreements with new members to establish an understanding that they will retire at a specified age, although older men on the same board are permitted to stay on until they voluntarily retire, or die.

The practice in one company for some time had been to "retain board members as long as they could walk and even longer," according to one of its top executives, and he thinks this has been detrimental to the guidance of company affairs. The company recently instituted a policy which prohibits the re-election of a board member after he has reached age 70. In at least two other cases, it was reported that the chief executive officer of the companies believed that indefinite retention of board members creates substantial problems in directing the company. These executives are endeavoring to modify the present practice of permitting outside directors to remain on the board indefinitely. One remarked that a man over 90 cannot be the active, energetic type of board member a company requires. Yet such a man is on the board and is in a responsible committee position, but there is no idea of moving him off the board because "this is not the nice thing to do."

* * *

The findings reported in this chapter show that there is a considerably more practical bent to the handling of retirement of executives than the mere observance of a mandatory or flexible retirement age policy. Where the realities of a current situation require the retention of a man, a company is likely to retain him. Retirement decisions are generally in the interest of achieving management continuity, which may demand the retention of special skills and talents. While most retirements occur at the normal retirement age, men are retained in employment or under some specific arrangements, according to the company's needs.

CHAPTER VII

Early Retirement and Preparation for Retirement

THIS CHAPTER EXAMINES THE REASONS executives voluntarily select early retirement and the effect such retirements may have on company staffing. It reviews next the problems that cause companies to initiate early retirement of executives, as well as the manner in which such retirements are handled. Also treated in this chapter are company practices directed to preparing individual executives for retirement, by encouraging them to face up to the personal adjustment that has to be made.

The close relationship between a company's retirement policy and its pension plan has already been referred to. The pension plan is often the instrument that shapes retirement policy, for the normal retirement age necessarily established by the plan is the age at which executive retirement most generally takes place. Benefits that accrue under the pension plan at that age represent the basic element in the retirement income provided executives. A pension plan also allows some flexibility with respect to the normal retirement age, by providing for retirement before that age, and these provisions have proved useful to companies in effecting early retirements where necessary.

There are some executives, however, who view with disfavor the idea of using early retirement provisions as the lever for effecting terminations. This reaction is understandable, in terms of the earlier purposes of pension plans, when a primary objective was to attract and retain capable personnel on a career basis, through to the specified retirement age. The reasoning was that the expectation of a pension keyed to length of service would tie employees to a company and thus discourage turnover. Provision for retirement before the normal retirement age was regarded as a concession to employees who might wish to retire early, and slight consideration was given to possible company interest in initiating early retirement. Companies were more inclined, in this earlier period, to accept and to bear with an older employee's inefficiences until he reached the retirement age.

Today, however, competitive pressures on companies are far more intense. The dynamics of industry demand the ultimate in efficiency at every level of an enterprise. To maintain an efficient management organization sometimes requires the separation of men before the time they would normally retire. When executive performance falls off to the extent of obstructing the management process or future staffing plans, companies may have to take action. The early retirement provisions of their pension plans provide a convenient and helpful means of removing men from jobs which they are no longer able to perform.

When early retirement at company initiative is considered necessary, companies generally undertake to aid the individuals concerned in preparing for and adjusting to their separation from employment. However, some men recognize their deficiences on the job, and they themselves seek early retirement, knowing that they will benefit by the pension plan provisions. Others voluntarily retire early, for personal reasons, even though their performance is entirely satisfactory.

A. VOLUNTARY EARLY RETIREMENT

Early retirement as a voluntarily selected objective has already been mentioned as being attractive to many younger executives. Whether finally decided on, or passed up, voluntary early retirement is a far more complicated personal matter than could be explored in the course of a study of corporate problems in retirement. However, it is clear that compensation levels and the adequacy of pension plans probably have much to do with whether or not an executive actually takes early retirement on his own initiative. In those companies where benefits are liberal and where, through pension, deferred compensation, bonus or profit-sharing plans, there are adequate reserves to permit early retirement, it is more reasonable for executives to expect to retire early than where plans yield minimal levels of benefits.

Comments of some executives made it apparent that requests by competent executives for early retirement are carefully reviewed, for they could be symptomatic of broad problems within a company. The reasons given for early retirement may indicate uncertainty on the part of individuals about their future in the company, or that compensation levels are inadequate. Companies recognize, moreover, that should voluntary early retirements become too widespread, an organization could be drained of valuable talent, which would complicate current and future staffing in major areas of operations.

Such a situation developed in one company in recent years to such an alarming extent that the company had to adjust its staffing arrangements to anticipate voluntary retirements before the normal age. Top executives of the company feel that, although turnover through voluntary early retirement may be healthy, a sudden change in the pattern it has now come to expect could signal future overstaffing. They are, therefore, vigilant in watching retirement age patterns for changes that may be developing.

Apparently, job pressures contribute to the desire of some men to retire early. Some companies reported that men in sales or marketing activities, or highly creative positions, get so engrossed in their work that a time comes when they feel compelled, for personal or health reasons, to withdraw from what has become frenetic activity on their part. But since men in similar positions in other companies do not seek early retirement, it cannot be occupational pressure alone that is determining.

Executives in many companies hold the view that early retirement is attractive to men with broad interests. Higher preretirement income permits savings and investments which, coupled with improved pension benefits, enables retirements long before they would have been possible in earlier years. There is no doubt, from examples cited in many companies, that executives engage in diverse activities outside the work situation, and frequently these become a consuming interest. When a man finds he does not have the time to participate in such activities to the extent he would like, early retirement becomes attractive.

One point on which there is considerable agreement

among companies is that where early retirement is voluntarily sought by a man, whether because of job pressure, or for other reasons, it is in the company's best interest to facilitate the early retirement. This is viewed in many companies as a form of "natural selection" which should not be interfered with.

Actually, voluntary early retirement at the executive level is not a pervasive problem. In fact, another study shows that seldom has the employment of executives terminated for reasons other than death or normal retirement.[13] In this study, no single case was reported in which voluntary executive retirement was so unexpected or such a blow to executive staffing as to cause serious problems. True, valuable men were lost, but it was reported in almost every company that it was possible to adjust to the loss, primarily because the executives seeking early retirement generally made their desire known well in advance of the time they planned to retire.

B. EARLY RETIREMENT AT COMPANY INITIATIVE

Almost all of the companies in the survey group have had to deal with ineffective or surplus executives at some time. The preponderant view in the field study companies was that where there are excess or ineffective executives, the problem should be dealt with aggressively, and this would mean early retirement. Where poor performance is clearly involved, attempts are made, before retirement action is taken, to stimulate an executive to better performance through suggestions or subtle proddings from above. Where such efforts are not

[13] Mabel Newcomer, *The Big Business Executive*, New York: Columbia University Press, 1955, p. 130.

successful, the individual is urged to voluntarily seek early retirement. This oblique approach in forcing early retirement makes it difficult to tell in some cases whether the early retirement of an executive is voluntary or company-initiated. Executives were reluctant to talk about cases of forced retirement, especially where a man had been a particularly valuable executive in earlier years.

One of the reasons for handling forced early retirements more or less secretively is that top executives believe that such retirements can have a deleterious effect on executive morale. In fact, it was reported in some companies that forced early retirement had resulted in concern among executives over who would be permitted to stay and who would be eased out. Generally, this state of affairs has been temporary, for it is said that once a company has completed the weeding out of poor performers or excess personnel, uncertainty among other executives dissipates. Moreover, many companies have found that, after early retirements have been effected, the remaining staff adopts a view that real attempts are being made to run a tight, profitable organization, and this is generally a stimulus to improved performance on their part. The significant practices followed by companies in forcing early retirements are reported below.

1. *Supplementing the early retirement benefit.* In one company the extent of the problem of unsatisfactory performance among executives led to the establishment of a special two-year program, designed to make early retirement attractive. Under this program an employee was required to take the initiative and voluntarily ask to be retired. An individual could be retired at age 60, or thereafter, with a pension equal to what he would have received if he had remained in employment through to the normal retirement age of 65. This is sometimes referred to as "making the man whole." The

company makes up, out of pocket, the difference between the early retirement benefits for which a man is eligible and the retirement income he would receive upon retirement at the normal age of 65, including social security benefits.

This plan for early retirement was not continued after the specified two-year period. However, the company would renew the plan, should poor performance again become widespread, or should there be an accumulation of excess personnel. The reason for setting a circumscribed period for voluntary separation, according to the top management, is that it provides an incentive for individual action that would not obtain if the special benefits were available routinely.

2. *Modifying the actuarial reduction of early retirement benefits.* In another company, older executives who are ineffective in their jobs are considered in one of two categories. The first includes those men who have slowed down because they lack motivation. The company feels it has a responsibility to do everything possible to help these men, by such means as transfer, assistance from younger men, or guidance from senior men. The second group includes executives who are "over their heads" in their present jobs, for whatever reasons. Attempts are made to interest these executives in early retirement, and this is not always difficult to do, because such men often want to "avoid the headaches" involved in trying to keep pace with their responsibilities.

The retirement plan in this company is so designed as to encourage early retirement, by making the benefits available to a man, if he retires during the five-year period before the normal retirement age, almost equal to what they would be at the time of normal retirement. This company follows a practice, which is fairly common among companies, of adjusting the usual actuarial reduction in determining early retirement benefits. While this reduction is normally from 7 to

8 percent per year of the normal retirement income, this company sets it in cases of forced retirment at 3 percent—some companies set it at 4 percent.

3. *Separation pay.* Forced early retirement is sometimes considered, in one company, for employees as young as 55 years of age; upon retirement the company provides separation pay and the vested portion of a man's pension. Executives over age 60 may be retired under this formula, or a more liberal one, based upon an appraisal of past performance, and a man's contribution to the company. The more liberal formula for men over 60 and under 65 years of age can yield for a man about the same benefit he would have received if he had remained in employment to age 65. At age 65, the pension plan benefits and social security payments come into effect and replace the company payments.

Separation pay is used in another company which, in recent years, has taken particularly aggressive action in forcing early retirement on ineffective excutives. Generally a man's ineffectiveness is first identified by some significant and obvious error in judgment, which shows up in the profit-and-loss statement for his department. Once a man has been recognized as a poor performer, his activities are closely observed. If he repeatedly makes errors the company forces his early retirement, and an executive severance benefit is provided. The severance pay formula provides an individual with up to two years of pay, which may be stretched over a four-year period. In addition, the man may defer his company pension until age 65, to thus avoid the early retirement discount and be in a more favorable tax position by leveling out his retirement income in the period before and after age 65.

4. *Arrangements by mutual agreement.* In three companies no actuarial discount of early retirement pension benefits is made when early retirement is decided upon by mutual

agreement between the company and an executive. Seldom in these companies, do retirements occur during the five-year period before the normal retirement age of 65 without a mutual agreement. Where a mutual agreement is not reached, it generally is because the company wishes to retain the man, but for some reason the man wishes to retire, even though he might suffer the full actuarial reduction in his pension (in one company he may also lose his deferred bonus). Mutual agreement is viewed in one of the companies as a fiction which camouflages forced early retirements that are in both company and employee interest. For the company, it avoids possible misinterpretation of action, and for the employee it preserves his social status and self-esteem.

5. *Budgeting early retirements.* In another company poor performance among executives is an extensive problem. It is estimated that among the top 30 executives in the company today, 18 were brought in from the outside to fill positions that were vacated by early retirements at the initiative of the company. In forcing early retirement, the company makes up the difference between the early retirement benefit and the benefit a man would receive if he stayed with the company to age 65. This is a costly program, particularly because of the extent of poor performance among the long-service executive staff. The company, therefore, allocates a specific amount of money each year as a percentage of its total operating budget to handle cases of poor executive performance. Top management feels that it is slowly, but surely, chipping away at a problem contributed to by changed business conditions which were never fully recognized by corporate staffing policies in past years.

6. *Disability retirements.* The provisions of disability insurance programs have been used by many companies as the means through which company-initiated early retirement

could be best handled. In one company this practice evolved when the first early retirements forced on executives were among men in poor health. Over the years the disability provisions have been interpreted so liberally as to permit forced early retirements at the company's initiative even when health was not the prime factor. Most of these companies have come to realize, however, that this is not the best way of handling their problems, and the practice has been less frequently followed in recent years.

C. PRERETIREMENT PROCEDURES AND COUNSELING

There was little question that the majority of executives with whom the matter of retirement was discussed generally do not relish the idea of moving from an active working life into retirement. In commenting on retirement, one executive said, "While you can philosophize about it, you don't have to like it." This reaction is generally more pronounced the closer a man is to retirement. It is for this reason that many scholars who are concerned with aging, and a few executives with whom the matter was discussed, feel that counseling can be valuable in helping a man to prepare for retirement and therefore help him to adjust to his retired role.

According to some executives, as well as a company medical director, counseling must begin early in a man's working life if it is to be effective at all. There is considerable disagreement over the value of counseling, for some believe that the very man who cannot find activities, health and contentment after retirement probably would not have been helped by counseling when retirement was imminent.

The view in many companies is that any arrangements preparatory to retirement are in reality preretirement counseling. Some executives also observed that preretirement counseling might be particularly helpful in overcoming executive resistance to early retirements in the best interests of a company. But, views on counseling are just as valid for the man who retires at normal retirement age. The several aspects of preparation for retirement are discussed below.

1. Conditioning Effect of a Fixed Retirement Age

The predominant view in companies with a fixed retirement age is that a most important value of a mandatory age is the fact that it conditions people to the idea of retirement. Mandatory retirement age is the point at which retirement *must* occur, and it is a constant reminder to a man to plan for his retirement. In contrast is the situation in companies with a flexible retirement policy, where men might not plan for their retirement, because the individual may not have knowledge in advance of the date at which he may be asked to retire. If the concept of the fixed retirement age does force a man to prepare for retirement, the likelihood is that the major proportion of his planning is financial. But, retirement counselors believe that mental conditioning is more important.

This matter of preparation for retirement was explored in discussions with older executives in the field study companies. The reactions of almost all of these executives were quite similar. They stated unequivocally that they are responsible adults, they know their company's retirement policy and when they will retire, and, therefore, should plan for themselves. It is their job to prepare themselves for retirement just as they had prepared themselves for other roles in life. Such preparation is viewed as a personal matter, not a company's concern.

Among the executives who held this opinion were several

who, in the past, had been exposed to some form of pre-retirement counseling. Their respective companies had experimented with counseling, but it had not become a continuing feature of retirement planning in the companies. These executives were somewhat more sympathetic than others to preretirement counseling, but they felt it would do much more good at lower levels of the organization than at the executive level. Moreover, they believe that for preretirement counseling to be accepted, it must come from a man who himself has experienced retirement. Among the field study companies, only one reported a formal preretirement counseling program for executives, although all other companies in the group follow some systematic procedure in anticipation of retirement.

2. Typical Preretirement Procedures

The procedures normally followed prior to a man's retirement are quite similar, so that one company's arrangements, which are fairly typical, serve to illustrate the principal procedural steps. A retirement committee consisting of five members of the board of directors, a member of the finance department, and a member of the industrial relations department is responsible for considering retirements, from two standpoints—in terms of the impact of future retirements on staffing, and of preparing for imminent retirements. Starting five years prior to each person's retirement date, the committee notifies the men who are approaching retirement, and their supervisors, of forthcoming retirements, and requests that employees select a retirement option made available under the company's retirement plan. Follow-up notices about retirement are sent to supervisors and employees one year, and then six months, prior to retirement. The committee is also responsible for the preparation of various symbolic awards to be presented upon retirement. These procedures are applied to all employees up through the executive levels.

Under the procedure, contacts with a man prior to retirement are limited to fairly routine matters. However, in discussion of retirement plan options, assistance in financial planning for retirement is offered, if the employee is interested. The major variation in these procedures among the companies is that notification and selection of options occur at different dates—in some companies, it is one year, or in others as much as five years, in advance of retirement, and in a relatively few companies, as early as 10 years before retirement.

3. Experience With Preretirement Counseling

In the only company found to have a formal preretirement counseling program for executives, it is an extension of the company's continuing program for providing guidance and counsel throughout a man's career. Executives meet in regular annual counseling sessions with members of the personnel department's staff or with an outside consulting psychologist. The preretirement phase of counseling comes into play at the time that an employee is notified about options available to him under the company's pension plan. In the case of poor performers, however, a man is guided toward thinking about early retirement if it is in the company's best interests to terminate his employment. It is believed in this company that counseling has helped men to prepare for retirement, and that the success of preretirement counseling is directly related to the acceptance of the technique well before specific counseling about retirement.

A small but significant group of companies reported

that they had considered preretirement counseling and were continually examining new programs in this field, although they had no current interest in adopting such a program. Some had, in the past, used the services of independent retirement counselors, university psychologists or special university classes designed to help men prepare for retirement. Generally, these programs were discontinued because the participating executives did not see real merit in the approaches taken, in comparison with their cost.

Where companies have experimented with and rejected counseling, the view is held that preretirement counseling activities are not successful because it is difficult to change people after a lifetime of conditioning. Moreover, there is a questioning of any practice that requires delving into the private affairs of individuals. From the experience in these companies a belief has evolved that any effort to counsel older employees should be carried out by specialized agencies or clubs *outside* the organization. For this reason some companies prefer to foster the activities of such groups where they can be helpful to older employees in plant communities. It is reported by the companies, however, that these programs tend to appeal more to employees at lower levels of an organization than those falling within the scope of this study.

Cost considerations have forced several companies that are interested in preretirement counseling to adopt a "do it yourself" approach. In one of these companies a series of meetings are held for employees at which retirement benefits are discussed and selected materials designed to be helpful in planning for retirement are distributed. This program comes into play at the time an employee reaches age 59, and some thought is being given to setting the age at 55. Five separate mailings of literature related to retirement problems are sent to the employee, in order to provide him with information felt to be important in retirement. The subjects covered include personal finance, living arrangements, adjustment problems, hobbies, and health factors. In addition, the company provides a subscription to a retirement journal which the employee may choose to get on his own initiative (the rate of acceptance and subsequent renewal have been almost 100 percent). Physical examinations are also provided older employees, and the resulting report is sent to the employee's home.

4. Over-all Views on Counseling

While companies in the field study generally do not provide preretirement counseling and only a few had experimented with it, the matter was discussed in all the companies. The consensus among executives interviewed is that at the executive level preretirement counseling is neither necessary nor advisable. If it is offered, it should be restricted to making available to a prospective retiree factual information that can be valuable to him. The argument that counseling involves a company too deeply in the personal lives of executives is a prevalent one. Moreover, executives feel that men with management status should be able to plan and adjust to retirement without preretirement counseling. It is felt also that preretirement counseling might carry the inference to older men that a company is preparing to ease men out of their positions, and at the executive level this could be particularly damaging to morale.

In a few instances, however, executives modified their views to allow that a company does have some obligation to help its employees adjust to their retirement, and that the demands of executive life, calling for a high degree of personal involvement in work, often prevent a man from planning for his retirement. These executives also point out that the necessary involvement of a company in an individual's personal affairs through its benefits plans, health examinations, etc., provides a basis for injecting counseling activities where needed. Considering individual reactions, it is seen as difficult to offer counseling on a selective basis. Moreover, executives speculate whether counseling might not result in a man becoming so overprepared for retirement that he would become ineffective during his last years of employment.

Underlying many comments on preretirement counseling is the general feeling that most forms of counseling are designed for the average employee rather than the executive. What may be needed at the executive level may be entirely different from what is needed at other levels of the organization, if counseling is needed at all. More meaningful than counseling, most executives feel, is for companies to use the years immediately before retirement to routinely call to the attention of all employees, including executives, the fact that working life is drawing to a close.

The only basis on which some companies firmly justify preretirement counseling is in connection with retiring excess or ineffective executives before the normal retirement age. There is a fairly strong minority opinion that preretirement counseling can be helpful when a man is about to be forced into early retirement. In such cases, the reasons for termination are more likely to be understood when explained on rational grounds, and thus it is possible to terminate men and retain their good will. Moreover, counseling in such situations can bring the ineffective man into agreement with his superiors that early retirement is best for him. Where the problem is one of excess executive personnel, counseling facilitates a reasoned explanation of the necessity for a man's retirement, relative to others.

The views and attitudes of the majority of executives on preretirement counseling are supported in the findings of Cornell University's "Study of Occupational Retirement." The following excerpts from an article based on this study are pertinent:

> . . . The findings suggest that *in every instance the two most important factors are an accurate pre-conception of retirement and a favorable pre-retirement attitude toward retirement.* Planning for retirement which is often cited as a main objective of pre-retirement counseling programs, is shown to be of relatively less direct importance. In fact, among those who lack an accurate pre-conception of retirement, planning impedes rather than facilitates adjustment; and it is shown to be related to successful creation of a role to fill the "retirement vacuum" *only* among those who hold a favorable pre-retirement attitude.
>
> * * *
>
> Evidence from the Cornell studies seems to show that the present generation of oldsters are more widely capable of managing their own lives than would be indicated by the proliferation of counseling programs, aids to self-help, advice to the "age-lorn," and organized activity programs *for* older people. Self-reliance such as this may not be the case with future generations, since the youngsters of today are fed liberal doses of the values of "playing it cool," of heeding one's peers in an "other-directed" manner, in short, of being "well-adjusted." Moreover, for those who are not "well-adjusted," professional help and advice springs eternal. Given this orientation, personal resilience may come to be relatively lacking, and *then* systematically "helping

people to help themselves" may be more squarely to the point—assuming there remains someone to help the helpers![14]

It may be said that no distinctly successful way of preparing executives for retirement has yet been found, if the experience of the field study companies is representative. Companies, on the whole, are dubious about the value of preretirement counseling in the preparation of men for retirement. Early retirement may be more easily accomplished after satisfactory preretirement counseling, but experience does not yet justify this conclusion. Counseling or periodic contacts with men prior to retirement can be helpful in moving men into retired status, but there is some question over what are the best or most productive contacts, in the interests of both the executive and the company. On the whole, experimentation in this field has left companies far from sanguine about their practices in preparing men for retirement.

[14] Wayne E. Thompson, "Pre-Retirement Anticipation and Adjustment in Retirement," *The Journal of Social Issues*, Vol. XIV, No. 2, 1958, pp. 43, 44.

CHAPTER VIII

An Overview of
Retirement Experience

COMPLICATED ADJUSTMENTS take place in handling retirement of executives, growing out of the interplay of
corporate and personal interests which surround the separation of men from an enterprise. On the one side is the
corporate objective of successful survival, based on the perpetuation of a sound, effective management team. On the
other side is the desire of executives to continue, regardless
of their age, to do satisfying and rewarding work in the
organization they have served for the best part of their careers.
One would expect a constant harmonious interaction of the
objectives on both sides. Yet they are often disparate, because
of the forces that bring change in the industrial environment
and in men. Trends of the times constantly necessitate evolutionary changes in staffing patterns, and retirement of executives is both a factor that causes change and a factor resulting
from change—sometimes it is a change in the company's
needs or it may be a change in the man himself.

161

In this chapter the more significant of these forces are related to the policies and actual practices followed by companies in retiring executives. The influence of patterns of policy and practice on the age distribution of executives also is reviewed, and the factor of retirement income in effecting retirements is considered. Experience with executive retirement in nonindustrial organizations is examined to determine whether their approaches offer constructive possibilities in relation to the problems presented to the business community.

A. RETIREMENT POLICY VERSUS PRACTICE

Myriad situations present themselves to a company in dealing with the retirement of executives, and in most instances the problems encountered could not have been foreseen. These unpredictable developments account largely for the policy shifts, innovations, temporary devices, and deviations from established policy reported by the companies studied, in their efforts to so handle the retirement of executives that neither corporate nor individual interest will be seriously damaged.

Looking over the total picture of reported policy and practice, in both the mail survey and field study companies, brings into focus the fact that, regardless of policy intent, there is, in practice, a high degree of variability in effecting retirements. Even where retirement policy is regarded as being rigidly applied, deviations from policy have occurred, or are allowed, because company action has to be realistic. It is shown below that categorizing companies according to what they actually have done, or are willing to do, in handling executive retirement, as against what they regard as their basic retirement policy, results in several departures from a simple two-part classification of mandatory or flexible retirement.

1. Policy Provisions

As shown earlier, retirement at a fixed age is the most common policy among the companies. It is found in 184 of the 228 mail survey companies and in 38 of the 46 field study companies. But considerable variations from policy have occurred in the practices of these companies. They indicate the extent to which corporations are forced to respond to their environment and other conditions that impinge on what they had expected to be a constant and unqualified policy.

While companies with a normal or mandatory retirement age regard this as most salutary in resolving problems of executive succession, a proportion of them provide, as a matter of policy, for exigencies which could require relaxation of the normal or mandatory age. The policies of 113 of the 184 mail survey companies with a normal or mandatory retirement age are designed to permit retention of men who have reached the specified age for retirement. Of these companies, 94 permit an executive to remain at work for "brief periods" beyond a specified retirement age, provided he continues to be able to perform his work and the company continues to need his services. In the other 19 cases, an executive could be retained indefinitely, so long as he is competent or is not immediately replaceable by a younger executive. Thus, over 50 per cent of all mail survey companies with a normal or mandatory retirement age consider it advisable to so qualify their policy that modification of the retirement age is possible. In the field study group, 26 of the 46 companies permit men to be retained after reaching the normal or mandatory retirement age—12 limit retention to "brief periods" and 14 allow indefinite retention.

2. Realistic Patterns of Practice

A seemingly inflexible policy of fixed retirement may take on a quite different character in application when it establishes an age for retirement and then allows variations that could postpone the retirement of some men. As reported earlier, companies actually have postponed retirements to serve corporate needs, even where policies did not so provide. Almost 60 percent of the total of 274 companies covered in this study—26 in the field study group and 124 in the mail survey group—have retained some men past normal retirement age fairly regularly for reasons considered of importance to the company. On the basis of their actual practices, it is reasonable to classify these companies, therefore, as being more flexible than rigid in applying the retirement age.

Various reasons were given for extension of service beyond the time retirement should occur, depending on the specific case, but in broad terms such action may be attributed to the emergence of four contingencies. The first is a shortage of personnel, either because of poor manpower planning or expansion of a business beyond anticipated levels. Second, forces beyond the control of the corporation come into play: war drains valuable men from the managerial and executive group, and thereby interrupts the orderly development of men through the ranks and eventually to the top jobs in an organization; general economic developments may interrupt the regular recruitment of men into the company each year. Third, through unexpected deaths, younger men may be removed as potential successors to older men. Fourth, there are the market and competitive factors which may make an older man valuable because of his special knowledge, technical training or personal contacts, and he has to be retained though he has reached retirement age.

Viewing company practice, rather than policy alone, results in a far different picture of corporate approaches in executive retirement. While no field study company handles retirements individually, as a *policy*, 13 of the mail survey companies do. Another 28 of the mail survey group and eight of the field study group stated that they have a normal retirement age yet allow deviations. But, when actual *practice* is examined in all companies, the number of companies that have applied the normal retirement age with flexibility, increases substantially—from 41 to 124 in the mail survey group, and from eight to 26 in the field study group. The handling of executive retirement will be considered, therefore, in terms of how policy is actually applied in practice.

The discussion below considers company retirement practices according to a five-part classification, presented in the order of the most flexible to the most rigid practice. Since company size might be regarded as the factor having the greatest influence on the determination of a company's retirement practice, the discussion indicates the size of companies found prevalent in each of the classifications. To satisfy any interest in possible patterns of practice according to industry, this factor also is dealt with. A detailed size and industry classification of companies according to their executive retirement practices is given in Appendix B.

In determining the degree of flexibility evidenced in a company's actual retirement practices, there are four factors that should be regarded as indicators of flexibility:

1. Retention as an employee beyond retirement age,
2. Retention as a consultant after retirement,
3. Retention as a member of the board of directors after termination as an employee,
4. Forced early retirement.

All of these practices indicate flexibility because, in each instance, separation of men from a company at the retirement age is modified, and it is reasonable to assume that this occurs to accommodate one or another objective in the interests of a company. However, the last three factors were not taken into account in the classification of companies here, and these exclusions must be explained.

With respect to retention of men as consultants after retirement, which is a fairly widespread practice, it was not possible to always distinguish between those situations where men are retained for reasons essential to the interests of a company and those where consulting arrangements are used to supplement retirement income, or for other considerations solely in the individuals' interest. For this reason, and because the retention of men as consultants after retirement does not in any way complicate planning for executive succession, this factor was disregarded in identifying a flexible retirement practice.

As to retention on transfer to the board of directors, this practice is relatively rare. Because continuation in employment within the executive organization is not always comparable with becoming a board member, and the number of these latter cases would not materially influence the distribution, this factor also was not considered.

In terms of the interaction of retirement policy and executive staffing needs, *forced early retirement* and *retention as an employee beyond retirement age* are clearly corporate tools in maintaining an effective management organization. These are the primary indicators of flexibility in retirement practice to serve company interests. However, most companies in the mail survey refrained from indicating whether they effect early retirement of executives when individual performance deteriorates; only 27 of them indicated that under certain conditions they do, or would, initiate early retirement. Although the field study companies freely gave this information, forced early retirement was disregarded as a feature of flexibility, in order to keep the classifications internally consistent. The companies are classified, therefore, only on the basis of the practice of retaining men in employment after the normal or mandatory retirement age.

Class A: No Normal or Mandatory Retirement Age. Companies in this classification do not have an established policy requiring the retirement of executives at any specified age. Frequently, this same individualized approach to retirement is applied to all employees in the companies. Among the mail survey companies, 13 are in this category. Of these, 11 employ 2,000 or more persons; the other two have under 1,000 employees. The companies do not cluster significantly in any one industrial classification, although four fall in the broad category of "manufacture of food and kindred products." Among these companies there is a heavy incidence of family ownership, and this undoubtedly influences the behavior of the companies in their retention of individual executives. None of the field study companies follow this extremely flexible retirement practice.

Class B: Normal Retirement Age But Indefinite Retention. The 28 companies whose retirement practices are of this nature permit the retention of executives beyond normal retirement age, so long as men remain competent and effective in their jobs. Actually, these companies establish a presumption that a man will be retired at a specified age, so that there can be no excuse at that time for not having a replacement ready to succeed him or, from a personal view, for the man himself not to be ready for retirement. However, if at the time of retirement the individual is still an effective executive, these companies see no reason why he should not continue to work as long as he is able. In these instances he is retained, though often in a different job from the one he had prior to the normal retirement age.

The companies comprising this group are generally somewhat larger than those which have no normal or compulsory retirement age. Each employs 1,000 or more persons—seven employing 20,000 or more persons. These companies are spread across the range of industry groups, with a cluster of 15 found in the industry groupings, "fabricated metals, electrical and general manufacturing."

Class C: Normal Retirement Age But Selective Retention. Companies that follow this practice do so for the same reasons as those given by companies that allow indefinite retention. However, although individuals may be retained after reaching normal retirement age, it is only for a brief period, or on a year-to-year basis. There are 109 companies in this group, and their approach represents the majority practice among the companies.

Generally, retention is permitted only where a man offers special skills, knowledge, or ability. Thus, the retention of individuals is on a *highly* selective basis, when top management feels that it is important for normal policy to be set aside. Where a person is continued after normal retirement age in these companies, it is most usually in a job other than his former managerial one, and typically as a consultant, technician, adviser or as a contact man with people outside the company. Generally, the managements of these companies do not view their retirement policies as even somewhat flexible. But their experience has been that it is frequently in the best interests of the company to delay certain retirements within the executive group on a selective basis for predetermined periods.

The large majority of these 109 companies employ 1,000

or more persons; only seven employ under 1,000 persons; and more than a third of the large companies are in this classification. Almost a half of the companies in the fabricated metals industry group permit selective retention, and these account for almost one-half of all companies that do so. The remaining companies are found to be in all of the several industries represented in the survey sample.

Class D: Mandatory Retirement Age Which May Be Waived. There are 47 companies which follow a mandatory retirement *policy* and waive it under only unusual circumstances. This group of companies actually consists of two subgroups, one of which requires retirement at age 65, and the other, at some later age. This classification is distinguished from the third category described above by the nature of the circumstances which will be recognized as so compelling as to permit an executive to be retained upon reaching the mandatory retirement age. Companies in this group would not retain executives because a successor was not ready, for that is regarded as an avoidable breakdown in management planning. But they would retain men in cases where war, death or other unusual circumstances would make it difficult to fill vacancies created by retirement, for such developments are outside the control of the company.

Some of these companies have not waived their policy since wartime shortages of managerial personnel made it necessary to do so. Others have waived the policy only rarely. All are concerned that departing from policy and permitting men to stay on might raise the presumption among members of the executive group at large that there is a possibility of being retained after the mandatory age. This is precisely what these companies wish to avoid. They are fearful that relaxation of their mandatory retirement policy, in other than clearly emergency situations outside the company's control, could undermine the over-all objective of providing for a normal turnover of executives through systematic retirement at a specified age. Eighteen of these companies indicate that early retirement has been, or would be, initiated when it is in the company's best interest to do so. A significant number of companies in the group are large companies and, but for this, their distribution by size and industry is not significant.

Class E: Mandatory Retirement With No Exception. A total of 77 companies have established and rigidly apply a policy of effecting retirements at a mandatory age, regardless of circumstances. This is the second most frequently followed retirement practice. This group also consists of two sub-groups, differentiated by the age established for retirement —at age 65 in one group; in the other, at some other age, generally age 68.

In many ways, companies in this group are the simplest to deal with in the framework of this study, because of the consistency in policy and practice they evidence. The companies typically report that holding to their rigid approach in the handling of executive retirement has been having constructive effects upon company planning, in making executive transitions, in maintaining the individual dignity of executives, and in opening up promotional channels within the organization. Among these companies, no deviations as to retention were found in the application of policy under *any* conditions since the time their policy was established. However, 12 of these companies have forced early retirement when men became ineffective in their jobs, or when changes in company structure resulted in excess executive personnel. These companies are spread across all of the industries represented in the mail survey. It is interesting that a number of small companies fall into this category, although this group consists mainly of large companies.

B. EFFECT OF RETIREMENT PRACTICES ON THE AGE OF THE EXECUTIVE GROUP

Three presumptions about retirement practices in the executive group were frequently expressed in the course of this study. One is that regardless of what a company says about its policy, there is considerable leniency in handling executive retirements, and so, executives stay on in employment far longer than other employees. The second is almost the reverse of the first, that is, executives have a greater financial ability to retire early than do other employees, and most of them do.

An indication of whether or not executives are generally retained in employment longer, or tend to voluntarily retire earlier, than other employees may be seen by comparing the age at which executives have retired with the age of retirement of all other employees. Data from 170 of the 228 mail survey companies on the average age of retirement of executives and of other employees permits a broad comparison, as shown in the following tabulation:

Retirement Comparison	Number of Companies
Relative to other employees executives retire—	
Earlier	44
At same age	68
Later	58
Incomplete data	58
Total	228

In 68 of the companies reporting, executives have retired at the same age as employees generally; in another 58, executives have, on the average, been retained in employment longer than other employees. In 44 of the companies there is a clear pattern of earlier executive retirement. It is interesting to find, in examining the individual company data, that companies showing the greatest incidence of early retirement of executives are those which tend to hold quite rigidly to a mandatory retirement age.

The third presumption is that where there is flexibility in retirement most executives would not retire at the normal age, and thus the executive group would be older than in companies where there is more systematic retirement of executives through strictly mandatory policies. "Is it true," one executive asked, "that in general there is a Tammany Hall effect in companies which follow a flexible retirement practice?" By this he was questioning whether executives are inclined to keep their cronies around them, and thus, typically, a flexible approach would mean an older executive group, because the older men would be reluctant to relinquish control within the company. If what he questions is actually so, it could be assumed, conversely, that the more systematic the approach to retirement, the more rational would be the distribution of executives among the various age categories.

These theories also could be tested from data reported by 224 of the companies participating in the mail survey, each of which specified the number of currently employed executives in given age categories. Approximately 22,000 executives were involved. These data permitted a distribution of executives according to age in companies where retirement practice is flexible, as against those with a rigid retirement practice, to thus determine whether flexibility in retiring executives has the effect of raising the average age of the executive group. The distribution is shown in the accompanying chart, where companies are grouped according to the earlier five-part classification, but with two of the groups refined to reflect differences in specific retirement ages among the companies. The definitions of the company groups shown in the chart are as follows:

More or less flexible practices

Group A: No retirement policy, complete flexibility;

Group B: Normal retirement age specified, with indefinite retention permitted;

Group C: Normal retirement age specified, with retention permitted on some stated basis, such as year-to-year;

More or less rigid practices

Group D: Mandatory retirement rigidly applied at age 65;

Group E: Mandatory retirement applied at age 65 except in cases of extreme emergency;

Group F: Mandatory retirement at age 68 or later, rigidly applied;

Group G: Mandatory retirement at age 68 or later, except in cases of extreme emergency.

In the chart, the percentage distribution of executives in each of the company classifications is shown for each age category. From this graphic presentation it is seen that, aside from men younger than age 40, there is a high correlation in the age distribution of executives within companies, regardless of retirement practices. This would suggest that factors outside of specific executive retirement policy and practice of companies are influencing the age patterns in the executive organizations. Conceivably, the promotional system helps

EXECUTIVE AGE PATTERNS, AMONG COMPANIES GROUPED ACCORDING TO THEIR RETIREMENT PRACTICES

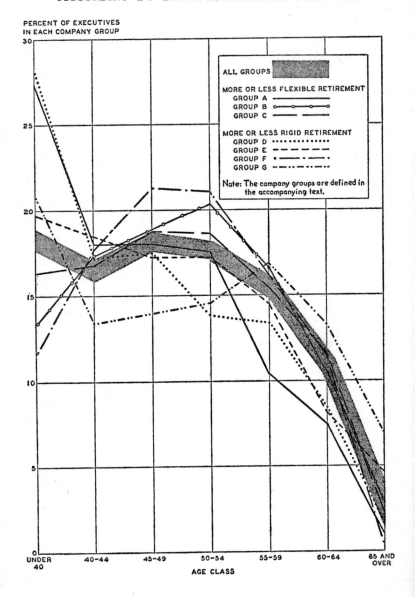

control age distribution, because of the length of time that elapses before a man is promoted. Additionally, it takes time for developmental programs to affect promotions. Physical and mental aging certainly are at work to force the curves in the chart to start turning down so dramatically beginning in the 55th year. Undoubtedly, these factors account in part for the relatively close ranges in which executives are distributed throughout the age groupings, especially later in life. The executive age patterns which the series of statistics might reasonably be expected to reveal do not prevail. For example, it might be assumed that companies in the "F" and "G" classifications would have considerably older workforces than other companies, because of the policy of mandatory retirement at age 68, but this is not so. While the "F" group of companies also follow this pattern for executives beyond the 65th year, the differences in age patterns between companies in this group and in others is not great. With respect to the "G" group, which is the smallest—accounting for only four companies with a total of 173 executives—a few individual cases clearly affect the over-all picture. What is shown in the chart is made especially clear in the following tabulation, which summarizes the data on which the chart is based:

Age Class	Distribution of Executives According to Company Retirement Practice	
	More or Less Flexible	More or Less Rigid
Under 40	16.5%	20.0%
40–44	17.0	16.2
45–49	18.8	17.7
50–54	18.9	16.7
55–59	15.4	15.5
60–64	11.2	11.0
65 and over	2.2	2.9

A remarkable degree of uniformity is apparent in the age distribution of executives among companies, regardless of retirement practices. The "A" "B" and "C" companies which are the more or less flexible, show a larger number of men, proportionately, in the 50 to 54 age group, but beyond that point there is a fairly comparable pattern among the two groups. The more rigid companies show considerably more executives at the youngest age level; but for that fact, the differences in the proportions of executives in age groups before the 50th year and after the 55th year are slight.

An examination of the data for individual companies shows few exceptions to the group patterns. Over all, retirement policies and practices apparently have no marked influence on the distribution of executives by age level within organizations. There may be the rare man retained far beyond the normal retirement age in companies, but the data show that he is rare indeed.

C. THE FACTOR OF RETIREMENT INCOME

Planning for retirement, as an aspect of maintaining effective management, must take into account the levels of retirement income available to executives. There is considerable evidence in this study that retirement income is a basic factor in the retirement or retention of men. Effecting separations through retirement, whether at, before, or after a normal retirement age, is made less difficult when a projected retirement benefit represents a satisfactory proportion of preretirement income. Companies in which levels of retirement benefits are relatively high have experienced less pressure for men to be retained in employment at retirement age, and much less of a problem with motivation of the elder executive, than companies in which the level of benefits is relatively low. Moreover, these companies are better able to arrange and gain acceptance of early retirement than companies whose benefit structures are less adequate.

Executives stressed the importance of adequate retirement incomes in effecting retirements. In companies where the ratio of pension plan benefits to final earnings is quite low, executives showed considerable interest in the proportion of final pay provided for executives under various pension plans. For this reason, such ratios were computed for selected companies in the field study group, and retirement benefits provided by five of these companies are shown in the tabulation below. The selection represents the extremes of practice among all field study companies, in terms of the least liberal and the most liberal benefit levels provided. Since career income affects benefit levels, the benefit formula of each of the five companies was applied to three income patterns.

Company	Pensions as Percent of Final Pay According to Three Income Patterns[a]		
	Pattern X	Pattern Y	Pattern Z
A	30.6%	25.6%	21.3%
B	41.6	35.4	30.0
C	42.9	36.9	31.6
D	56.3	55.0	54.0
E	60.3	55.2	50.7

[a] Pattern "X": steady increases in pay have occurred throughout the executives' careers. Pattern "Y": increases have been steady for a time and then were more highly progressive. Pattern "Z": more rapid increases occurred, but quite late in a man's career.

In companies "A," "B" and "C," where retirement income as a percent of final pay is well below 50 percent, some difficulty has been experienced in the retirement of executives. In two of these companies, retirements always occur at the normal retirement age, because the company takes a firm stand against requests for retention beyond the normal age. In the other company there is considerable retention of executives and, among those who are forced into retirement at the normal age, there has been much dissatisfaction.

In contrast, companies "D" and "E," have had a distinctly favorable experience in moving men into retirement at times most opportune for the company. In one company many executives are retained beyond the normal retirement age, but there are also many terminations through forced early retirement, when this is in the best interests of the company. The other company has never retained men beyond the normal retirement age, but has had to force early retirements, when extensive terminations were required as the result of a widespread program of cutting back company personnel, including the executive staff.

Pension benefits do not, however, represent total retirement income. Over two-thirds of the 228 mail survey companies provided information based on *total retirement income,* including social security benefits, pensions, deferred compensation, and payments under employment and consultant contracts after withdrawal from full-time active service, but excluding income from other sources, such as stock options, stock purchase or thrift and savings plans. The tabulation on the following page summarizes the data reported by these companies on the *ratio of total retirement income to average final five-year earnings,* covering 1,750 retired executives.

The retirement income of the largest proportion of executives retired from the reporting companies amounts to from 30 to 50 percent of their average earnings over the last five years of their employment. In a significant proportion of cases, however, retirement income is from 50 to 59 percent of final average earnings. Despite this pattern, a high proportion of the mail survey companies report that one of the major problems they see for the future in handling executive retirement is to find ways of improving retirement benefits.

Retirement Income as Percent of Average Earnings	Percent of Retired Executives
Less than 10%	0.3%
10-19%	4.7
20-29	12.4
30-39	23.6
40-49	26.5
50-59	22.0
60-and over	10.5

The experience in both groups of companies shows that, in general, adequate levels of retirement benefits make possible company action that otherwise would be difficult to achieve. Many companies are alert to this factor and have used the pension plan as a positive incentive to maintain or improve executive performance through to retirement. In one of the field study companies, the plan is seen as stimulating performance, not as a shelter for poor performance. Its pension benefits are based on the average of the last five years of earnings. Well before the five years preceding retirement, an executive and his superior establish a retirement income objective. It is then possible to calculate the income level which the man must reach in the five years prior to retirement if he hopes to get the desired retirement benefit. However, since income increases only on the basis of exceptional performance, a most realistic and understandable incentive is provided for the executive. This plan clearly illustrates the relationship between retirement, a pension plan, and executive motivation.

The stimulus of the retirement benefit on the attitudes

of executives brings the discussion of executive retirement in almost full circle. There is a pragmatic element in the retirement process. Companies' needs and executives' needs must be considered if retirement policy is to provide for management continuity and the orderly retirement of men without conflict.

D. RETIREMENT EXPERIENCE IN NONINDUSTRIAL ORGANIZATIONS

The experience of the companies in dealing with executive retirement shows a similarity of problems and solutions to them, although they may arise out of different background situations. Retirement at the executive level in a company can be likened to the retirement of policy makers or other important individuals in nonindustrial organizations. Executive retirement practices in several such organizations are reviewed below.

1. The Military

The retirement system for officers in the United States Army—and in the other military services—is closely tied to its promotional system. Through its approach, the Army fulfills two main objectives: separation of officers judged least qualified, and retention of those who show the most promise and ability. The Army policy is designed to retain an aggressive organization by weeding out those who are not judged capable for promotion, and this evaluation occurs at scheduled periods based on length of service in a given rank. This policy of promotion or separation is referred to as "up or out" and may be characterized as both rigid and flexible.

It is rigid in that some officers *will be retired* at certain ages, because there are more men available than vacancies. After a specified number of years in rank, an officer is either promoted, or he is separated from active service. It is flexible because while some are retired, others are retained and promoted.

The key to the system lies in the selection of those deemed best qualified for continued service. Special selection boards of officers make the decisions on promotions on the basis of standardized annual efficiency reports, with respect to each officer on active duty. These reports—a combination of subjective comment and numerical scores—give a picture of each officer's capabilities as well as his weaknesses. Since, over the years, each officer is rated by different supervisors, and in a variety of assignments, it is believed by the Army that the accumulated reports provide built-in cross checks on ratings among superiors. Although highly formalized, the system is flexible enough to allow exceptions. The Army recognizes the need to retain men with special skills, even though the officer may not be worthy of promotion according to the usual criteria.

The Army feels that it is highly successful in isolating, in any officer group, the 10 percent extremes of best qualified and least qualified. Beyond the initial selection of officers from these two groups for promotion or separation, there is general agreement that selections are difficult to make, but they are made, and with an impartiality which Army personnel feel helps morale. The over-all system is viewed as one which minimizes resentment and frustration in the lower echelons, because it is impartial and because it assures lines of promotion being kept open.

Assuming that an officer is not separated but promoted on schedule at each step in his career, his normal retirement date is known to him years in advance. Normally, an officer retires as a colonel five years after achieving this rank, which is generally at age 55, but based on his age at the time of earlier promotions, retirement can occur as late as age 59, which is the terminal age. Only a relatively few men go beyond this grade to the rank of general officer. The officers who do, however, may remain in the service under a deferment by the Secretary of the Army until they reach age 60. A major general may be retained until the age of 64. Thus, under the Army system, only a five-star general is continued on active duty after age 64; the terminal age for officers is 59, when, as a colonel with no promotion to a general officership available, a man retires.

The relationship recognized by the Army system between succession and retirement is comparable to that found in industry. The major difference, however, is that the constant transfer and rapid movement of men through the Army organization makes possible a series of appraisals on which the retirement or promotional action is based. There is, however, a certain degree of artificiality in the system, for in the interests of forcing a man up or out, more reliance is placed on length of service than on ability, in a majority of cases. This appears to be the conclusion of a Defense Department committee which, from the results of a study of the military, concludes that officer promotions in the future should be based on ability as well as service.[15]

Although larger industrial companies may base executive appraisals on evaluations of performance by several superiors, it is difficult to imagine a general company practice providing for transfer and rotation with the frequency typical of the Army system, or that length of service alone could be so controlling. Obviously, the nature of work as-

[15] "Pentagon Would Drop Seniority and Push Ability," *New York Times,* January 6, 1961, p. 8.

signments at the executive level in industry do not permit the same degree of executive interchangeability in jobs. Management demands great ability and creativity in work, which in turn requires that a man be given time to make his contribution to the organization. These are far different requirements from those of the Army, where a man's value may derive from familiarity with procedure and detail, which comes from long service.

2. The Federal Civil Service

The Civil Service Commission is forbidden by law to discriminate in federal employment on the basis of age. The majority of federal jobs have no established age limits, and no mandatory retirement age. However, retirement becomes automatic at age 70 if an employee has had 15 years of service, but an employee entering federal service at age 60, for example, can continue in employment until age 75.

The retirement system of the government permits a number of retirement arrangements for employees. For example, an employee with 30 or more years of service can retire voluntarily at any time between the ages of 55 and 70, with a reduced annuity. Even after age 70, he may be re-employed on a year-to-year basis. Since a civil service annuitant's retired status is no bar to further employment in the federal service, according to law, a retiree may be hired to fill any job for which he is qualified. For the majority of annuitants who are re-employed, the annuity continues without interruption, but at a reduced rate, during the period of his re-employment. Thus, the retiree receives his annuity when he is not working, and a combination of annuity and reduced salary equal to full pay for whatever time he does work.

This liberal retirement policy is further individualized

by use of a tapering-off system, where possible and desirable. Before actual retirement age, an employee may work out with his immediate superior an arrangement for a systematic gradual transition from a full and heavy work schedule to retirement. In co-operation with the particular agency, an employee may seek part-time rather than full-time work, or his work schedule may be rearranged in order to reduce physical and mental pressure on his job. Both of these arrangements are predicated on the individual remaining active in his agency. There is current interest by public administrators in a plan for combination of pension and part-time pay, which would further encourage tapering-off procedures. Under the proposal, federal agencies would be allowed to adjust the work schedule of employees prior to retirement by utilizing accumulated leave, or by having the employee work part time, in order to provide a taper-off arrangement while retaining a normal level of income. Alternatively, some thought is being given to permitting an agency to arrange to re-employ an employee after his retirement on either a part-time or full-time basis. This would formalize present informal arrangements, in that they could be planned prior to retirement.

The approach in the federal civil service is obviously controlled by the legislative prohibition against discrimination in federal employment on the basis of age. Moreover, it applies to employees at all levels of service. Problems of "deadwood" may exist in federal agencies, but this is outside the scope of this review of federal retirement policy. It is the taper-off arrangements that are interesting. They appear to offer a considerable degree of flexibility, which can be especially valuable in jobs where men are engaged in technical and professional rather than broad administrative positions. This is comparable to the many arrangements existing on an informal basis in industry, as already reported, and could be of real interest to some industrial employers for those types of jobs which can be easily compartmentalized, or which do not involve continuing and long-term managerial responsibility.

3. The Tennessee Valley Authority[16]

In 1933, the Tennessee Valley Authority was established as a separate agency of the federal government, but without coverage by the social security or the civil service retirement systems. In 1939, the Authority established its own retirement system, with retirement optional at age 60, and mandatory at age 70.

By 1954, TVA recognized an emerging problem, because employees generally were remaining in employment until age 70, when they were obliged to retire. In studies conducted by the TVA, the majority of employees indicated that inadequate income was a primary reason for remaining in employment, but a general distaste for retirement was also involved. The management saw this as a serious situation. Because of the indefinite retention of older workers, younger efficient people were laid off when reductions in force became necessary.

Based on the studies, the TVA retirement plan was revised in 1957. A pattern of selective retirement was provided for by establishing a normal retirement age of 65, with extension of employment, one year at a time, at the option of the management, up to age 70, which remained the compulsory retirement age. An extensive preretirement coun-

---

[16] Based on correspondence with the Tennessee Valley Authority, and on an article by E. B. Shultz, "Selective Retirement and Preretirement Counseling in the TVA," in *Industrial and Labor Relations Review*, January, 1959, pp. 206-213.

seling program was introduced, and pension benefits were increased materially. These changes were designed to make voluntary retirement before age 70 more attractive, and to lessen resentment in cases of automatic termination by the management at age 65.

The selection procedure followed at age 65 requires a review of the physical condition of an employee, and a judgment by the director of his division as to the desirability of his retention for not more than one year, in light of (1) his work record, (2) the need for his continued service, and (3) his physical condition. In cases of retention an employee is given a one-year temporary appointment, which is subject to termination in case of reduction in the workforce. The new system also recognizes the need to judge each case according to the staffing needs of a particular division. Such factors as the need for special skills, the over-all number of older workers, and the possibility that retention will block a younger man's promotion are considered.

After three years' experience, TVA officials express satisfaction with the revised retirement program, and, perhaps more important, they detect a favorable change of attitude toward retirement on the part of the employees. However, relatively few management people have been retired under this program.

The TVA system is somewhat similar to a retirement plan found in one of the field study companies, except for the fact that age 68 is the terminal age in the company. These approaches to handling extensions of employment after men reach a normal retirement age are interesting and may be adaptable in company formalization of retention practices, provided that the conditions in a company permit adherence to the normal retirement age for the majority of cases.

4. Other Organizations

Retirement practices of other organizations examined during this study are not especially significant for industry except for the many illustrations provided of certain types of productive activity in which performance is not necessarily affected by age. In church organizations, retirement is generally informal, and it is presumed that a man will work indefinitely, although some churches have established mandatory retirement ages for certain assignments. In schools and universities, there is a range of practice. Some require mandatory retirement at a specified age—largely state supported schools and colleges—but in many other instances, it is the administrator rather than the professor who must retire at a specified retirement age. In the professions, where men are primarily self-employed, medicine and law are practiced indefinitely and are under no compulsion to retire from their work at specified ages. In political appointments, the number of older men in responsible positions at all levels of government in the United States and abroad is legion.

Over time, men in these types of organizations, professions, and occupations, and in the arts, have worked well beyond the ages normally considered in business to be the terminal age for employment. One most interesting illustration was related by the dean of a law school who for years has deliberately employed on his faculty men who have been retired from other institutions. The dean himself was age 46 when he initiated the practice. He cited the fact that at age 67 Charles Evans Hughes was engaged in working for a foundation for nothing, when he was told that, even though he worked without compensation, he had reached the retirement age in the organization—which evidently could not be violated. Pointing out that Mr. Hughes was appointed Chief

Justice of the United States in the following year, the dean remarked that he "held the job with great distinction for eleven years after having been found to be too old to work for a foundation for nothing!"[17]

The interesting feature in relating retirement to these occupations is that they indicate some degree of variation in individual ability to make a continuing contribution to society. Perhaps life span is related to occupation. But whether certain types of people select certain types of occupations or whether the occupations themselves have an influence on the people is not known. What is known, however, is that some people work creatively and constructively at more advanced ages than others, and frequently they are professional people.[18] The experience of the companies suggests that this is already recognized by the formal as well as informal retention arrangements made with engineers, scientists and other professional people, where retention would not necessarily interrupt the normal development and promotion of men within the management organization.

[17] Will Lissner, "Life Begins At 65 For Law Faculty," *New York Times*, January 4, 1961, p. 35.
[18] Dublin, Lotka, Spiegelman, *op. cit.*, p. 7.

CHAPTER IX

Retired Executives Report Reactions to Company Policy and Retirement

EXECUTIVES WHO HAVE RETIRED FROM A COMPANY are the only group who have been exposed to every aspect of a company's retirement policy. They have observed retirement policy in application prior to their own retirement—as it affected subordinates, colleagues and superiors—and have experienced the impact of the application of policy on themselves. They also have already faced up to deciding upon the activities to be pursued upon retirement. For these reasons, questions were raised with retired executives about company practices and retirement, with three main objectives:

1. To explore the views of retired executives about the retirement practices of their former companies, in terms of their reactions at the time of retirement and in retrospect, now that they have been in retirement for some time,

189

2. To determine their current viewpoints with respect to retirement in general, and whether their experiences in actual retirement have changed earlier opinions,

3. To discover what activities retired executives have engaged in since their retirement.

Before turning to the analysis of responses, some facts should be given about the 205 participating retired executives, as a group. The retirees were formerly associated with a total of 14 of the field study companies, which fall into nine industrial categories. Two of these companies have rigid mandatory retirement policies; 11 others, which also have mandatory policies, allow exceptions that result in some flexibility in effecting retirement; only one of the companies handles retirements on a somewhat flexible basis.

At the time of reporting, the largest proportion of the group of retired executives—slightly over 50 percent—had been in retirement from one to three years, and about 15 percent, for from four to six years; another 15 percent had been retired less than a year, and the remaining 20 percent for various periods in excess of six years.

Information on the length of time retirees had been employed in their respective companies was reported by all but one of the 205 retired executives. The periods of service vary considerably, but the weighted average service for the entire group is 36.7 years. By far the greatest proportion of retired executives had been with their companies from 35 to 45 years (115 retirees), and 25 of them had more than 45 years of service; of the remaining 64 retirees whose service was less than 35 years, 45 had served for 25 years or more.

Addressing themselves voluntarily to broader questions than executive retirement practices alone, many retired executives indicated a deep concern for the manifold issues involved in retirement—personal factors as well as broader sociological questions—but generally within a framework of company interests.

A. VIEWS ON RETIREMENT POLICY

It would be understandable if it were found that evaluations by retirees of the retirement policy followed in their former companies had been conditioned by their reactions to their own retirement. But this was not the case. In general, retired executives say the policy followed in their former company is a satisfactory one in terms of company interests. When any reservation was expressed about the handling of retirement, it related not to an individual company's policy specifically, but to the bases on which retirement is determined in general. In no case did the responses from an individual indicate a violent reaction against the company because he had been retired at a particular time or age. In large part, there was a careful evaluation of individual versus corporate problems in the handling of retirement, and a differentiation and understanding as between what a man might like and what is best for a company. In terms of the company's interest, three areas of comment are particularly significant, and these relate to retirement age, transfer of executive responsibility to successors, and executive effectiveness.

1. Retirement Age

The vast majority of the 205 retired executives reported they had retired at the company's normal retirement age. Of the group, 146 retired at the normal age, 39 retired before the normal age, and 20 remained in employment for some period after the normal retirement age.

The 20 retired executives who were retained after the normal retirement age had been employed by five of the 14 companies. Three of the companies had employed 17 of these men. It is interesting to note that these three companies all follow a somewhat flexible retirement practice of permitting men to be retained beyond normal retirement age when, and for as long as, the company's best interests are served. The other two companies involved recognize a (more or less) fixed retirement age, yet have retained three men after the normal retirement age; however, seeing that 18 other retired executives participating in the study had retired from these two companies at the fixed retirement age, the retention of only three men appears to be the exception rather than the rule in the companies.

A total of 142 of the 205 retired executives indicated, in response to open-end questions, what their views are toward a mandatory versus a flexible retirement policy. The concepts expressed do not generally reflect a reaction against the policies under which they were retired. An analysis of the retirees' attitudes toward a mandatory retirement age is given in the tabulation on the following page. The quantification among the 142 executives is based on the reasons given for the particular attitudes expressed.

Of the 142 retired executives who gave their reactions to retirement policies, 93 volunteered the information that they agree with and support the idea of a specific mandatory retirement age for executives. The reasons cited for holding to this opinion are varied, and coincide largely with the reasons given by active executives who support mandatory retirement, as reported earlier.

As seen by 49 of the retired men who uphold a mandatory retirement age, its greatest value is the opportunity afforded to promote younger men to more responsible positions which are opened up through the retirement of older men. These promotions are seen as being important in terms of retaining men, but also because of the improvements in the management staff which result from the advancement of younger executives. It is interesting that so many retired executives retain the continuing interest in the management process that their comments indicate.

Reactions of 142 Retired Executives Toward Mandatory Retirement	Frequency of Reaction
Support mandatory retirement age	
Allows promotion of younger men	49
Older men lose efficiency	10
Eliminates need for selective retention	6
Although arbitrary, selective plan would be worse	7
Total	72*
Basically for mandatory retirement, but—	
Favor post-retirement consulting arrangement	19
Favor "tapering off" of employment	4
Total	23*
Against a mandatory retirement age	
Chronological age improper standard	7
Rejects valuable experience and contacts	18
Selective retirement plan favored	30
Retention in employment as consultant desirable	6
Total	61*

* Several executives gave more than one reason.

One retired executive commented on the promotion of younger men in most positive terms, and his observations reflect the attitude of the majority who regard this factor as of prime importance. He stated that younger men "bring in newer ideas, stronger drive, greater incentive. The older men live in the past, always talking about what they did 25 years ago. Let the younger men run the show—and for their time period they will do a better job than we could do." Adding to these concepts, a retiree holds that the responsibilities, tensions and pace demanded of executives in recent decades have been such that "men just burn out or die before their time."[19]

Other reasons given by the retired executives in justification of mandatory retirement are that (1) older men lose their efficiency, and a fixed age for retirement removes such men automatically; (2) a fixed retirement age relieves executives of the onerous responsibility of deciding when others should be retired; (3) although a mandatory age is arbitrary, selective retirement would be worse. While agreeing basically with mandatory retirement, 19 retired executives would have liked a post-retirement consulting arrangement with their former companies, and a few individuals favor a tapering-off of active service for a few years before actual retirement.

One argument for a mandatory retirement age is particularly pertinent, for it coincides with the concern so often shown by active executives over preserving individual dignity in the application of retirement policy. A retiree pointed out that without a mandatory retirement age most people would be prone to think, from year to year, that they have "one more good year left," and that this is likely to go on "until illness or death intervenes." He feels that, worse yet, ". . . our employer would have to tell us our days of usefulness are over," and he considers that a "blow to pride," which is avoided when the retirement date is pre-established.

On the other hand, 49 of the 142 men who commented

[19] In this connection, see also Edwin E. Wagner, "Differences Between Old and Young Executives on Objective Psychological Test Variables," *Journal of Gerontology*, July, 1960, p. 298.

on retirement age reported they are opposed to rigid adherence to a specified retirement age in a company. They favor a more selective plan, which would permit the retention of executives who demonstrate they are able to continue to provide efficient service. It is the feeling of most in this group that methods could be worked out for the retention in employment of older executives, in consulting or other capacities. Many who argue along this line would have liked to stay on in employment, and a small number were actually retained beyond the normal retirement age. Throughout the comments of these retired executives runs a strong recognition that methods must be found for advancing younger men, but that the wisdom and experience of older men should not be lost entirely.

Suggestions for consultancy arrangements, for boards of elders to advise and counsel, or for various taper-off programs were repeated many times in the responses. Retirees who would have liked to lengthen their employment find it hard to be reconciled to the fact that, up to the minute of a man's retirement, he is considered able to work effectively but, overnight, he is no longer needed. Shouldn't there be a mechanism, some retired men question, to permit executives who reach a specified retirement age, and yet are able to contribute an extra year or two, to remain in employment without distorting the retirement-succession cycle. This reaction to retirement policy in general is similar to that of most active executives.

Among the retired executives are some, however, who reject consultant or other arrangements as a means of prolonging employment beyond the normal or mandatory retirement age. One executive referred to some of these arrangements as "planned subterfuges" to keep men on the payroll, and he holds that retention of the older men interferes with the younger men who have been moved up to more responsible positions. A few others are of the same mind, although they expressed their opinions less explicitly. They were, however, forthright in saying that no exceptions should be made to the fixed retirement age and, in one case, that the value of the skills of older executives is "greatly exaggerated." An executive stated that, from his observations in his former company, it is generally executives who have the least to offer who wish to extend their employment, while the more able men are generally "ready to step aside."

Retirements before a company's specified retirement age were reported to have occurred because of poor health in 12 cases, or were the choice of the individual himself in 23 cases. It is noteworthy that 24 of the 39 men who retired early had been associated with companies that reported a practice of initiating early retirement whenever that course is believed to be in the company's best interests. This may reflect the success some of the field study companies have had in their planned programs of getting executives to step forward and voluntarily request early retirement, as a method of "preserving a man's dignity."

2. Transfer of Responsibility

The retired executives generally view the retirement policies of their companies as having largely solved the problem of arranging for planned transfer of executive responsibilities from men facing retirement to their successors, and thus achieving continuity of management. There is an interesting consistency in the beliefs concerning retirement policies and practices among the several retirees of a company, regardless of whether it is a company with a fairly fixed retirement age or one which exercises considerable flexibility in handling retirement.

It has already been noted in an earlier chapter that there is some degree of conditioning of attitudes about retirement on the part of active executives. The same sort of conditioning appears to be carried forward after retirement. Retired executives know their companies. They are informed about the reasons for various company actions or at least feel that, based on prior knowledge about the company, they can speculate about the reasons for company actions with some degree of precision. Thus, a deviation from policy which permits one man to stay beyond the normal retirement age may be annoying to the man who is already retired, but the deviation is usually rationalized. The majority of retirees, though no longer personally involved in executive staffing patterns, are still able to see clearly the interrelationships between retirement practices and the perpetuation of the management organization.

In considering the need to assure continuity and effectiveness of management, the retired executive generally believes that for the well-being of the company, executives are retired at about the right age. There are 141 retired executives who hold this view. Another 50 of them believe that executives are retired somewhat earlier than is necessary. It is interesting to find that almost a third of this smaller group were employed in companies where the level of the pension benefit, in terms of the ratio to final pay levels, is relatively low. In interviews with active executives in these companies, a strong interest was found on the part of some to remain after retirement age in order to build up additional retirement benefits. Only 11 retired executives believe that retirement occurs generally at too late an age. Three executives did not give their views on this point.

Given the fact that such a large proportion of the executive group believes that retirement occurs at about the right time, it is not surprising that almost all of the same executives reported that their replacement was ready to take over their job at the time of their retirement. In 130 cases, the now retired executive feels that at the time he retired his replacement was ready to do the job to which he would succeed. Another 25 executives reported that a replacement was ready one year before the date of their retirement, and 24 reported that they felt the replacement needed another year of training before being ready for the promotion.

There seems to be a fairly general trend of thought running through the responses from the retired executive group that the meshing of retirement and the transfer of responsibility occurs with relative ease and with considerable success in the majority of company situations. This is probably largely the result of an attitude reflected in the comments of many of the retired executives that the greatest responsibility of an executive is to pass his knowledge on to others so that upon a man's retirement no break will occur in company operations. As one executive said in his comments, "Changes have been rapid and drastic in industry in recent years, and it is a severe test of the adaptability of an older person to adjust to such changes. If he can pass on to others the fundamentals which will always be basic, he can step out with the knowledge that he has left behind what he has learned." This is a laudable objective, and, to the extent that it permeates the thinking and actions of men in the executive group who are approaching retirement age, the perpetuation of effective management will more likely be achieved.

3. Executive Effectiveness

There is a paradox which constantly recurs in the comments of retired executives. Most of these men subscribe to the soundness of their former company's policy in systematically retiring older men. But many of them are equally firm in their conviction that generally there are additional years of able service left in a man at the time of his retirement. Yet they generally acknowledge the fact—and see the attendant difficulties—that although some men are able to continue to work, some men are not; and that still others lose the capacity to perform at satisfactory levels even before reaching the normal retirement age. Evaluation by the retired executives of the abilities of executives who had retired from their former companies at the normal or mandatory retirement age is pertinent in this matter.

Of the 205 retired executives, 163 made such evaluations. Among these, 22 hold that during their last five years of employment, all executives whom they saw retire at normal retirement age, could have continued serving their companies effectively for another three years, granted that no unforeseen health problem arose during that period. Only 21 of the retired executives feel that, of the men who retired in the five years before they themselves did, none could have continued effectively in employment. The others (120 retirees) all feel that some proportion of the men could have continued to be effective executives, and almost one-half of these reported the conviction that over 50 percent of the executives who were retired were still capable and efficient.

Retired executives were also asked to comment on the problems they had observed or faced while active in their companies, with respect to men in the executive group who had ceased being effective executives. Fifty-nine executives reported that during their careers they had observed executives nearing retirement age who were not doing their jobs as effectively as they should. But in only 12 instances did the now retired executive recall that ineffectiveness among his immediate subordinates had caused operational problems. In most cases, therefore, the problems were seen in other departments or activities than those for which the particular executive was responsible.

B. REACTIONS TO RETIREMENT AND RETIREMENT ACTIVITIES

The fact of retirement affects executives differently. For some, retirement may be the beginning of a new and exciting period and is approached with anticipation. For others, it may be a numbing experience, as it terminates old associations which have been a prime source of stimulus and satisfaction. There are also those who face up to retirement realistically, preparing for it financially and philosophically, and are ready to and capable of making the most favorable adjustment possible.

As already noted, an acceptance of the need for systematic retirement practices is typical among the retired executives, and there is no significant difference in views as between men who had been retired for less than a year and those who had been in retirement for over 10 years. Even men who would have liked to remain active in employment at the time of retirement understand that the retirement-succession relationship precluded it. This is clearly not an attitude of self-sacrifice, but signifies rather what may be a salient factor in executive success—the subordination of personal desires to company interests. As one retired executive observed: "All these old executives who die of boredom in retirement show just one thing—they are one-track minded and were not executive material to start with."

Though the retirement process, as related to maintaining

effective management, is understood and accepted by retired executives, there is on the whole a deep questioning of many of the basic assumptions behind retirement policy, in a broader frame of reference than individual company retirement practice. A sentiment that threaded through the comments of retired executives, whether they uphold or oppose mandatory retirement, is that the chronological age standard is wrong. As shown earlier, many retirees hold that its application discards valuable experience of still capable men and valuable personal contacts they have built up. This is regarded as a loss to their companies and frustrating to the individual executive.

Some men apparently feel that there should be a way to distinguish men who are retired from those who are discharged. After all, they argue, the retired man is not personally at fault for having been retired—he has only reached an arbitrarily determined retirement age. This point was cited in one of the field study companies, in the case of an executive who on retirement lamented that thenceforth there would be nothing, in terms of his title of "former vice president" to distinguish him from a colleague who had been fired. This man tried, therefore, to interest his company in creating an honorary rank of "vice president emeritus," but his efforts were unavailing.

With respect to the timing of their own retirements, the general reaction among retired executives is that retirement occurred at about the right time. However, views on what is the right time for retirement appear to have changed slightly between the actual time of retirement and the time of this survey. There are 160 executives who reported that, at the time of their retirement, they had believed that they should have been retired when they were; but only 140 of these men still felt, at the time of the survey, that they should have retired at the age they actually did. This is interesting, especially in light of the fact that only a small proportion of the group who reversed themselves indicated in retrospect that *at the time of their retirement* they would have been willing to stay on in employment.

Of 192 retirees who responded to the question of whether they would have liked to remain in employment at the time they retired, only 91 replied affirmatively; most said they would have liked to stay for periods of from one to three years; some, for four to seven years; and a few, for periods of eight years or more. But 101 men reported that *when they retired* they had no desire to continue in employment.

C. RETIREMENT ACTIVITIES

With respect to satisfactions or problems found in the years after retirement, 106 of the retired executives made no comment whatever. Of the remaining 99, the great majority (84 executives) reported that they were satisfied with or enjoying retirement. A few are exultant over the freedom they have for family, fun, travel, and cultural activities; others are getting satisfaction from rendering service to civic and charitable enterprises which, one retiree pointed out, are unable to "afford salaries commensurate with the responsibilities required by such agencies." Several of these retired men view retirement as a period for enjoying life, and as a well deserved reward for decades of hard work. Fourteen retirees reported they have been philosophical about being retired, but are not necessarily liking it. It is noteworthy that only one retired executive said he is unhappy in retirement, having found it difficult to fill up the time he has at his disposal.

The retired executives have been engaged in a wide

variety of activities since entering retirement. The following tabulation summarizes the information on retirement activities reported by 195 executives:

How Retirement is Spent	Number of Retirees
Total leisure	
By personal desire 31	
Because of ill health 26	
Total	57
Paid employment	
Full time 12	
Part Time 16	
Unspecified 31	
Total	59
Philanthropic work	79
Total executives reporting	195

Almost one-third of the 195 retired executives have been engaged in paid work (59 retirees), although only a small number of them reported that they had actively sought employment. One of these men had retired from his company before the normal retirement age, and contemplates retiring from his present job when he reaches age 65. The types of employment engaged in by the retirees include employment in executive positions in companies, social organizations, and universities; in law or medical practice; in a business club, a retirement counseling firm, and a travel agency; in civil defense, and with the federal government. Several retired executives have their own businesses or are in partnership with others; one is a rancher. Some are part-time business consultants—three for their former companies. A few retirees reported they had been offered employment, which they refused.

Besides those retirees who are enjoying total leisure—mingled with chores around the home, in some cases—a high proportion of retirees stated that they have not looked for or wanted paid employment because they wished to be free of any such responsibility. These latter men constitute the large majority of the group of 79 retired executives who give their time free to agencies needing their services. Their activities range from membership on boards of trustees of hospitals, to work with groups of retired people in local communities. In a few cases, retired men have been providing advisory services to local governmental bodies or to the federal government. Evidently poor health and aging have not generally been deterrents in terms of preventing retirees from seeking employment. Only 26 retired executives reported that these factors have so hindered them; some of the group nevertheless have engaged in philanthropic work.

Many retired executives who devote their retirement years to personal pleasures, and even some who have been employed since retirement, feel that retirement should be enjoyed without having to engage in work and cope with the responsibilities a person faces in work situations. In their comments, many executives who have not been actively engaged in work, or who would not want the responsibility of a full-time job, report that they would welcome ways to render service to their former companies, even if it would be only in the role of a consultant. This desire on their part apparently stems from a belief that their specialized skills would be of greatest value to their former employer. Thus, while work in general may not be attractive, work at the old job might be.

Of the retired executives who specified the kind of work they have engaged in since retirement, whether on a full-time or part-time basis, most have been in activities outside the field in which they had worked prior to retirement. In general, these men report that they have found their new work challenging and, in some cases, far more demanding than the retired executives actually desire. The fact that some executives find post-retirement work burdensome provides a basis for speculation about the types and extent of work activities which would appeal to a group of retired executives over a long period of time.

In only a limited number of cases were comments made about retirement incomes as a factor in retirement life. Three retirees regard their former company's retirement benefits as rather inadequate, relative to preretirement income, and considering mounting living costs. Only one retired executive who has engaged in paid work said that supplementing his retirement income is one objective in working, because his retirement income is inadequate. Several other retirees indicated, both directly and by implication, that retirement income has been no problem, some regarding their company retirement benefits as liberal. In fact, one retiree made a point of saying that the retirement job was taken to satisfy his need "to keep busy," not because of income, for his company's retirement plan "is good." One retired executive who described his retirement as being "most pleasant," spoke of having "somewhat of a guilty feeling that I'm getting so much and presently giving nothing material, at least of a sacrificial nature, toward the rewards."

*　*　*

Retired executives react to the problems connected with the interrelationship of staffing and retirement policy in much the same way as the active executives in their former companies, and in other companies. The parallels in the thinking of the two groups are remarkable. There is a strong segment of opinion among the retirees that the age standard for retirement is arbitrary and that individual abilities should be taken into account. While giving recognition to the difficulties of individual selection for retention, many retirees consider it unfortunate that an executive is retired only because he has reached a given age, though he is still able to work effectively. Apparently, these retired men are saying, as some active executives have, that what is needed is the discovery of a formula or method for determining, objectively, when a man ceases to be able to continue to work effectively, rather than at what age he should retire.

There are those whose concern goes beyond the impact of policy on the individual. They deplore the fact that current retirement practices restrict utilization of the talents of a highly skilled group of men who can contribute to society at large, but who in retirement status may have little opportunity to do so. This issue is outside the scope of this study, but it is clear that one of the broad social problems in this field concerns methods of using the skills and talents of retired persons, even though it might not always be possible to do so within the framework of active employment in the corporate situation.

CHAPTER X

Executive Retirement in Perspective

CONTRADICTORY FORCES ARE AT WORK in the nation at large, and they affect the retirement practices of corporations. On the one hand, the retention in the future of men beyond normal retirement age may seem inevitable, because of the ebb and flow in the supply of men with the potential to become managers and executives. This supply of high talent manpower tends to condition current views of retirement policy at any given time and may, in the long run, determine the specific policy applied in any company.

On the other hand, the dynamics of a business may necessitate changes in executive staffing patterns, leading to a reduction in the number of men in executive positions. This development derives from deep changes that continually affect the manpower needs of industrial organizations. Already, changes in operations, products, or markets have made it necessary for many companies to retire executives long before normal retirement age, because such changes have resulted in an excess of managerial personnel. Moreover, as the processes of industrial activity become ever more complicated, companies find that it is difficult for some men to keep pace with the demands of a growing and changing enterprise, well before they reach the normal age of retirement.

Broad trends in the national economy impose curious strains on company policy, and they imply conflict between executive staffing and retirement policy, which makes necessary the consideration of retirements in the light of company needs at specific times. This in turn implies greater variability in handling retirement in future years than has been the general development in the recent past. These factors have been evidenced in the findings of this study.

A. SUMMARY OF FINDINGS

The experience of the companies with executive retirement reflects in large part the many pressures that have come to bear on company policy and practice. Summarizing this experience in a concise series of points is made difficult therefore, and thus it is not attempted. Instead, the major issues in executive retirement and the significant approaches taken by the companies are drawn together and presented below.

Executive Retirement and the Management Process

1. *Underlying company practice in the retirement of executives is the objective of assuring continuity of effective management, in the long-run interest of the enterprise.* To

this end, the majority of companies shape, adjust, or revise their practices to meet the challenges imposed by the constantly changing times. Moreover, companies demonstrate by their practices that retirement policy must contribute to planned and orderly staffing of the management organization, and to high morale and motivation among executives.

2. *Management generally recognizes the sensitive balance required in applying retirement policy, in order to achieve optimum ultilization of executive talents by motivating all executives to maximum performance throughout their working life.* Almost all executives contacted during this study saw clearly that the administration of retirement policies can contribute to or undermine individual performance. It is not surprising to find, therefore, that companies attribute great importance to the relationship between retirement practices and the staffing of the executive organization, as a matter of corporate survival.

3. *Dealing with executives in the application of retirement policy has in general been on the basis of understanding and concern for the interest of both the individual and the company.* This could be a cold, arbitrary and impersonal matter but this is not typically the case. Though successful company survival is a prime management concern, this has not led to arbitrary and impersonal treatment of executives. Some executives are disturbed about their retirement, and the way they feel they are being treated as they approach retirement. However, the majority are not; even among retired executives there is an understanding of the need for retirement policy, even though it has forced them into an inactive status. They largely support the retirement practices under which they retired. This suggests that executives tend to be conditioned by the practices with which they have lived, or have even helped to develop, over the years.

4. *One of the chief concerns of top management is how*

to assure that all executives retain interest and enthusiasm in their work, through to the age of retirement. Top executives are far from complacent over the general understanding of retirement policy, for they realize that policy alone will not achieve their desired objectives. Companies with a mandatory retirement policy do not believe that, because such a policy tends to force retirements to occur systematically, it will also *automatically* insure satisfactory attitudes among executives and effective planning for succession. Even where a flexible retirement practice is followed, rarely has a company permitted the practice to drift unchecked and result in the indefinite retention of men, without regard to the demands of effective current and future staffing.

5. *The relation of retirement to overall staffing, succession and the transfer of responsibility is inescapable.* Future staffing requires understanding of the manpower needs of a company, in terms of projected growth, and it also demands planning for retirement. When men are available for future assignments as others retire, there is a continuity in the management of the enterprise. But there is an additional and incremental value in relating retirement to staffing. If men in an organization understand the relationship between their own retirement and the preparation of their successors, a more effective transfer of responsibility upon retirement may be expected. The retirement of men and sequential promotion of others is a conditioning process within an organization. Older men look at retirement as inevitable, and younger men come to learn, understand and accept the need for the organization's preparations for the impact of retirement, long before they are themselves affected.

Decisions about retirement, whether directly or indirectly, are always related to staffing questions. Will a delayed retirement disturb plans for executive promotion? Is a delayed retirement necessary because of an unforeseen vacancy in the organization? Is the retention of a retiree as a consultant going to have an effect on active executives? When early retirements are forced does this shake the remaining staff, or, alternatively, will executives react against the fact that they have to carry ineffective men? All the companies have had to deal with most of these questions at some time in their handling of retirement.

Administering Executive Retirement Policy

6. *The need to actively oversee retirement policy administration is generally well recognized by companies.* Fitting retirement policy to the needs of many diverse situations, without disturbing executive morale, requires administration attuned to the realities of the world in which the corporation operates. There is nothing static about the business environment. It is not surprising, therefore, that new demands imposed on executive retirement policy have ultimately led to departures from stated policy, as revealed in the actual retirement practices of companies. These differences between policy and practice are reflected in the corporate practices of retaining men in employment after reaching retirement age, or as consultants, or by forcing early retirement.

7. *The traditional, simple concepts of flexibility or rigidity in categorizing corporate approaches to executive retirement are no longer truly descriptive in the light of this study.* The most prevalent approach to executive retirement establishes a fixed retirement age at which all executives are expected, and expect, to retire. But attached to that age is a degree of variability that permits a company to separate men, or to retain men, whenever it is in the company's best inter-

ests to do so. But to do this, it is recognized that some preparation of men and the organization is necessary. Retirement policy based on this concept is viewed by companies that take this course as being rigid by its own terms, in that deviations from the normal retirement age are determined by some current company necessity rather than the personal desires of individuals. It is also viewed as flexible by others. But terminology is not important. What is important is that retirement policy be geared to the real needs of companies.

Executive Retirement Decisons

8. *Early retirement can be one of the most important factors in maintaining the tone of the executive organization, but decisions in this area are among the most difficult to make.* In the eyes of some men, being forced into retirement is tantamount to termination. In fear of this reaction, there is a sympathetic attitude among the executive group at large, and a consequent reluctance to force early retirement on a colleague. But, when necessary, the decision has to be made, and company experience shows that forcing retirement can have a constructive and stimulating effect on an organization, if such action is not arbitrary but is clearly related to the realities of a company's situation.

The several reasons for early retirement are that there is an excess of executive personnel, that poor performance has arisen from poor health or other reasons, or that a man himself wishes to withdraw from a company. Where early retirement is sought by executives, the corporate problem may be a loss of valuable skills and talents at a time when the organization has no replacement available. In such cases, companies may find it necessary to make continued employment attractive, through bonuses or salary increases providing current or deferred income.

Early retirement at company initiative is a far different and more pervasive problem. One could imagine that forcing retirement on individuals could result in concern and uncertainty throughout the executive staff; however, in only one company in the group did this develop. Early retirement due to ineffectiveness has been found necessary to spark performance throughout the executive organization; this probably suggests to executives that top management is looking for peak performance. Some of the questions that have to be raised in making a decision on early retirement are summarized in Appendix C.

9. *Although early retirement can be expensive because of the financial arrangements generally made, many companies regard the cost of keeping a poor performer on the payroll as being greater than the cost of early retirement.* The financial arrangements made between a company and executives to facilitate their early retirement take various forms, and the approach taken in effecting early retirement also differs among companies. Some periodically offer to supplement early retirement benefits for all who step forward and voluntarily take early retirement. This procedure is seen as valuable, in that it obviates the onerous task of identifying and dealing with problem cases, even though effective as well as ineffective men may seek early retirement. The limit placed on the duration of the programs minimizes continuing uncertainty among the executive staff as to their own security. But in most companies, exclusive reliance on the voluntary approach would be considered untenable, because of the strong conviction that the continued employment of poor performers is detrimental to the organization and to the morale of the executive staff. Generally, therefore, retirement

is forced on a man when he identifies himself by the sub-standard quality of his performance.

10. *While decisions on early retirement are difficult because of the effect on the men and on morale, decisions to retain men after the normal retirement age are difficult because they may undermine retirement policy and thus affect the organization at large.* No doubt this explains the wide interest in arrangements for tapering off the involvement of older men in the executive process, as against retaining executives in employment as consultants, when they come to the end of their working careers. Perhaps, too, this explains the variety of views on how to continue to hold a man to a company as a consultant or adviser. Some in management have envisaged the possibility of organizing boards of senior executives with an advisory role to provide a background of business philosophy to younger executives. These executives, removed from direct responsibility, could give guidance and counsel to younger energetic men who might otherwise go off in wrong directions, without considering all aspects of a problem.

Despite the attractiveness of these ideas, a problem arises when a man is retained in employment. Retention is an action which can disturb an organization because other executives may infer that they have a chance to be retained, despite admonitions to the contrary. In final analysis, therefore, when a company decides to retain a man, it has to weigh subtle reactions to retention, and the possible precedents which may be established, against its need for the man. The conclusion always depends on *judging* whether or not retention is a necessity from the company's standpoint. Some of the questions involved in making this decision are also summarized in Appendix C.

11. *Consulting arrangements with retired executives provide a variable tool for management, in that it can be*

molded to fit a variety of situations. Retention of retired men as consultants is sometimes arranged in companies which follow a mandatory retirement policy as a method of keeping a man available without violating retirement policy. But, it is also utilized in companies where fairly flexible approaches are taken to the retirement of executives, either because it is not until after an executive has been retired that the company has some special and unexpected need for his services, or because the executive is interested in moving from full-time to part-time employment, or to employment for a specific task. The selectivity afforded by the consulting arrangement overcomes the objections to a rigid retirement policy, for it permits the retention of men without weakening retirement policy or threatening the dignity of a man who is not retained. Consultancy also enables a company to provide incremental retirement income, without disturbing over-all retirement arrangements.

Consulting arrangements, however, can also have negative values when viewed from the perspective of certain executives. The consultant may interfere directly with the work of the man who succeeded him. The older man's physical presence may inhibit his successor's actions or even disturb relationships between the now responsible executive and his subordinates.

12. *Procedures for the preparation of executives for retirement have not been extensively developed among the companies, probably on the presumption that executives are better able to prepare themselves for retirement than are other employees.* This inference appears to be substantiated by active executives as well as by several of those who have been retired for some time. Both active and retired executives see some shortcomings in company preretirement practices. First, preretirement procedures and contacts with older

executives have been too routine and mechanical to be of value. This is especially a problem where there is interest in forcing men into early retirement. Second, over-all procedures are designed for the average person and do not permit dealing with the questions and problems of any one individual in meaningful terms. Third, where factual information about retirement is available to an executive, it is generally left to the man to ask for it, and he might not do so.

These points highlight two extreme views about preparation for retirement. According to one, preretirement counseling, advice and information should be routinely provided, regardless of rank. According to the other, the company should take a more passive role by standing ready to assist only if asked to do so. From the comments of executives, including the retired men, there is no question that men of executive stature favor the latter approach over any organized program designed to prepare the executive for retirement.

B. CONCLUSION

There is a certain mystery about the executive process and what makes one man so much more successful than another. Thus, it is understandable that when an effective executive organization is brought together, so much importance is given to the reactions of individual executives to company policy. Among the reasons cited for the particular approach to executive retirement followed by a company, whether mandatory or flexible, was executive reaction, which is reported by the companies as influencing morale and ultimately the quality and level of performance.

When an executive who has been successful in his job

and important to his company approaches his retirement age, it is difficult to see him prepare to leave and then actually separate from the organization. This state of affairs prevails even in companies where mandatory retirement is the rule. It is as though an individualized approach to executive retirement would, therefore, be preferred to other approaches, yet several factors make a policy of individualization difficult to maintain.

One of the most compelling of these is the difficulty of deciding in each case when retirement shall occur. Another, is the degree of certainty that is demanded in staffing arrangements at the executive level. Even in companies taking a flexible approach, it has been found that there is value in establishing a general age at which retirement will usually take place, although variations may be permitted. Without such arrangements, future staffing would be typified by a most random pattern.

Individualization would remove the retirement process from the controls that should apply in a majority of circumstances. All men are not uniformly able to continue to contribute to the well-being of a company upon reaching normal retirement age. But an individual approach raises the presumption that any man who wants to stay would be permitted to do so, yet not all have a contribution to make beyond a normal retirement age. It could not be assumed that an executive would respond to suggestions to retire under an individualized approach because of the emotional connotations involved. Most executives, therefore, would be challenged, even those who have always placed corporate interest above personal interest.

There are arguments, however, that would support a policy of retaining executives beyond what is currently regarded as a normal retirement age. A most popular one stems from a growing interest in the concept that mandatory retirement has an unfortunate effect on the economy and can be detrimental to a business. From the national point of view, the argument is that the existence of an older and retired population means that it is necessary for the younger population to support the older group. The question is raised as to why older people who are still able to work should be retired, thereby creating a drain on the productivity of the remaining people in the population. Even for the corporation there is possible loss when an older man with special abilities or knowledge is retired.

Retention of executives beyond specified normal retirement age may become necessary in the future because of the steady increase in the proportion of older people in the population of the United States. Data on age and occupational distribution show that almost 55 percent of the proprietors and managers, and over 35 percent of professional and technical workers, in today's labor force are 45 years of age and over. It is estimated that by the end of the present decade these two groups will grow significantly—professional and technical workers by over 40 percent and proprietors and managers by about 22 percent. With each year, the relative proportion of people aged 45 and over is increasing, and is expected to continue to grow.[20]

These facts have serious implications for management staffing. An estimate for 1970, of employed persons who will be in the age group of 35-44 years, is only about 19 percent. Contrast this with the situation in 1960 when the proportion in this age group was over 22 percent.[21] By 1970, while there will be a larger proportion of older persons in the workforce, there will be an appreciably smaller number of

[20] United States Department of Labor, *Manpower—Challenge of the 1960's,* Washington: Government Printing Office, 1960, p. 18.
[21] *Ibid.,* p. 6.

younger persons entering the age groups from which, in the main, executive manpower during that decade will be drawn. It is reasonable, therefore, to envisage for the 10-year period starting in 1970 a situation in which, unless there are revolutionary changes in management staffing requirements, there will be a shortage of manpower from which future managers can be drawn. Such a situation may demand the retention of managers beyond the retirement ages considered normal today.

Manpower developments, national productivity, and a growing public opinion about the aged and their problems must be taken into account in long-run executive staffing and retirement. Typically, public reaction is either for or against—it does not distinguish by recognizing subtle issues involved, such as the differences between one class of employees and another, or between who is truly capable and who is not. There is a popular belief that longevity gains have been significant, even though this is not the case, and that they should be recognized in determining retirement age. Evaluations of corporate policies and practices by executives themselves, as well as the public, give considerable weight to this popular idea about longevity. If, therefore, a mandatory retirement age were to be universally followed, there could be public reaction against this. Yet, if retirement determinations were entirely individualized, pressure would inevitably be felt to permit more than a selected few to stay on in their assignments, regardless of ability to adjust to new methods and techniques and to continue to be effective employees.

The number of retired people is large and growing. They are an easily identifiable block which political leaders have courted and will continue to court. Thus, regardless of sound corporate practice, public opinion and pressure may grow to demand that corporations re-evaluate retirement practices.

Executive retirement as understood in the corporate setting has to be viewed in a broader framework than simply the retirement of men at the end of their working careers. There is a bond between executive retirement and the management process. This is the major finding of this study. Filtering out the details of the practices in companies, a possible evolution of retirement practice is seen, calling for a recognition of the problems with which companies are confronted. Realistic company practice is compounded of four elements:

1. *A specified retirement age,* based on general understanding and acceptance within a company that retirement occurs at a specific age at all levels within an organization. Company actions must be directed to gaining adherence to this so that both the company and the individual can anticipate and, therefore, plan for retirement.

2. *Early retirement,* as a means of retaining an effective management organization. Company-initiated early retirements can be arranged whenever it appears to be in a company's best interest to do so. Benefits can be provided to minimize employee hardship, on the basis of a formula that considers the quality of past service, and this in itself provides stimulus to effective performance whether or not the company's interest will at some time be served by early retirement. Voluntary early retirement may not be in the best interests of a company, but it can be controlled.

3. *Selective executive retention,* to gain flexibility in application of retirement age at the discretion of a company. This would enable a company to retain men for specific periods—as employees or consultants—depending on their ability and capability, and the need of the company for their

services. Retention for a specified period is desirable, for this places a terminal date on the relationship, which can always be renewed if it is in the best interest of the parties.

4. *Accountability and responsibility* can contribute realistically to motivation and morale and to sound executive retirement. If an executive who is held accountable is not performing satisfactorily in his job, early retirement would not come as a surprise to him. If an executive retains a subordinate beyond the normal retirement age, he should be responsible for explaining the reasons for this and why a replacement is not available.

* * *

Executive retirement might be considered as being far removed from the challenges corporations face in today's world. This is not so, because of the changes constantly pressed upon corporations. Change is the rule, and it is occurring faster today than at any other time in the history of industrial society, for technological innovation continues at an accelerated pace, and corporations are competing on an international scale to an extent never conceived of in past years.

Changes in competition demand new ideas, new approaches and, frequently, new people. It demands an ability to move with the times, in fact, ahead of the times. The management organization must, therefore, be typified not only by a systematic approach to retirement, but also by a higher degree of selectivity than ever before, in terms of the ability of corporate managers to bring and hold together the executive group most capable of dealing with new products, machines and methods. This will mean a pattern of executive retirement at a specified age for the majority. It will also require, however, new staffing patterns which will call for individual treatment of some executives, leading perhaps to the early termination of some and to the retention of others. In each case, the decision would be based entirely on the ability and availability of individuals to make a real and continuing contribution to an enterprise.

APPENDIX

APPENDIX A

Detailed Definition of "Executive"

THE WIDE VARIETY in size, structure and activity of the many companies asked to participate in this study precluded any arbitrary and firm definition of the executive group. The following comments were used as guides in identifying "executives" in each company, as follows:

a. They are the highest paid employees, and in numbers probably constitute about 1 percent of the normal total number of employees in the company.

b. They include all or almost all the individuals in the highest four levels of management responsibility on the corporate organization chart.

c. Regardless of title, they usually fill such functions as:

Chairman, president, executive vice president, top marketing executive, top manufacturing executive, top financial executive, assistant to president, top industrial relations executive, general sales executive, top advertising executive, top engineering executive, top product research executive, treasurer, controller, secretary, top legal executive, top purchasing executive, top foreign operations executive.

Major sales executive at the division, region, product or district level, or in charge of export sales, sales promotion or marketing research.

Ranking executive or major functional assistant at major plant, factory, works, mill or refinery.

Major corporate specialist in construction or maintenance, industrial engineering, equipment design, product development, process research, research and development, patent or other law specialties, insurance or tax matters, credit and collection, general accounting, cost accounting, budgetary control, internal auditing, scheduling, quality control, personnel administration, labor relations, management development, industrial health or safety, public relations, government relations.

APPENDIX B

Distribution of Companies

I N THIS APPENDIX, the 274 companies participating in this study are distributed according to size and industrial classification. They are also grouped according to the retirement practices followed by the companies as classified in Chapter VIII. The definitions of the classes shown in this tabulation are as follows:

Class A—No Normal or Mandatory Retirement Age

Class B—Normal Retirement Age, but Indefinite Retention

Class C—Normal Retirement Age, but Selective Retention

Class D—Mandatory Retirement Age Which May Be Waived

Class E—Mandatory Retirement With No Exceptions

COMPANIES DISTRIBUTED BY SIZE AND
EXECUTIVE RETIREMENT PRACTICE

Number of Employees	Company Class*					Total
	A	B	C	D	E	
Mail Survey Companies						
Less than 499	1	..	..	..	..	1
500-999	1	..	7	3	5	16
1,000-1,999	..	2	10	4	7	23
2,000-4,999	5	6	19	12	14	56
5,000-9,999	5	7	25	4	19	60
10,000-19,999	1	3	18	4	14	40
20,000 or more	..	3	11	5	13	32
Total	13	21	90	32	72	228
Field Study Companies						
Less than 499	..	..	..	..	..	..
500-999	..	..	..	2	..	2
1,000-1,999	..	1	..	..	..	1
2,000-4,999	..	..	4	..	..	4
5,000-9,999	..	..	2	2	..	4
10,000-19,999	..	2	2	3	3	10
20,000 or more	..	4	11	8	2	25
Total	..	7	19	15	5	46
All companies	13	28	109	47	77	274

* See definition on preceding page.

Companies Distributed by Industry and Executive Retirement Practice

Industry	Company Class*					Total
	A	B	C	D	E	
Mail Survey Companies						
Food and kindred products	4	2	9	3	5	23
Fabricated metals, electrical and general manufacturing	5	13	38	12	23	91
Chemicals, petroleum, and rubber ..	2	3	15	6	15	41
Electric, gas, transportation, and communications	2	2	10	6	17	37
Finance, insurance and real estate ...	..	1	14	5	9	29
Miscellaneous	..	..	4	..	3	7
Total	13	21	90	32	72	228

* See definition on page 227.

COMPANIES DISTRIBUTED BY INDUSTRY (Continued)

Industry	Company Class*					Total
	A	B	C	D	E	
Field Study Companies						
Food and kindred products	..	1	2	3	..	6
Fabricated metals, electrical and general manufacturing	..	2	9	3	1	15
Chemicals, petroleum, and rubber ..	..	2	4	6	1	13
Electric, gas, transportation, and communications	..	..	2	2	1	5
Finance, insurance and real estate ...	..	1	1	..	2	4
Miscellaneous	..	1	1	1	..	3
Total	..	7	19	15	5	46
All companies	13	28	109	47	77	274

* See definition on page 227.

Checklists for Systematizing Retirement-Retention Decisions

WHAT ARE THE QUESTIONS which should be asked by management when it considers the early retirement or the retention of an executive? Although some of the relevant questions are posed below, it should not be presumed that any one situation will directly parallel another or that the conclusion that a man must retire or must be retained will be any easier to make because these questions have been considered and disposed of in one way or another.

The questions are designed to aid in gathering both the information and the judgments which should be helpful to management in concluding about early retirement or retention. But they obviously will not provide a precise basis for decision in any specific situation. The need for a final judgment is inescapable.

I. Early Retirement Checklist

1. Has the question of early retirement of the individual been raised because of—
   a. His health?
   b. Poor performance on his part?
   c. He is obstructive to change?
   d. His position is no longer essential?
2. Who has raised the question of early retirement? Is he in a position to know the work of the executive for whom early retirement is suggested?
3. Is the suggested action based on an isolated instance of poor performance, or on continuing evidences of incompetence?
4. What are the results of appraisal of recent job performance, in terms of—
   a. Teamwork,
   b. Leadership and organization,
   c. Initiative,
   d. Contribution to profit,
   e. Decisiveness—reaction to crisis,
   f. Technical competence?
5. What steps have been taken, when, and with what success, to encourage the individual to recognize and correct his deficiencies? If no steps have been taken, why not? What steps could be taken now? Who should be responsible?
6. What has been past practice in similar cases at comparable job levels in the company?
7. What skills, talents, and interests does the individual have, which are not being fully utilized in his present position?
8. Could a practicable change of assignment challenge the individual and thus stimulate better performance?

9. Is the man involved in any current projects which would be seriously delayed by his separation, and should that factor influence the timing of his actual retirement?

10. What is the situation regarding a satisfactory replacement—
    a. Replacement immediately available,
    b. No replacement needed,
    c. Specified time required for preparing replacement?

11. Would any problem in management manning be created by the transfer of a replacement?

12. Is it likely that the executive, if retired, would find employment with a competitor? Is this a disadvantage? If so, can it be minimized?

13. What precedent would be established, strengthened, or broken by early retirement of this individual?

14. What might be the impact of this specific early retirement on—
    a. Superiors, including the board of directors and major shareholders,
    b. Subordinates and co-ordinates,
    c. Suppliers,
    d. Customers,
    e. Competitors,
    f. Community relations?

15. What is the mental and physical health of the man based on—
    a. Recent history,
    b. Current situation,
    c. Prospective problems?

16. What are the apparent attitudes of the executive toward retirement, considering—
    a. Marital situation,
    b. Realistic planning for retirement,

    c. Personal adjustment,

    d. Degree to which the individual's future social position depends upon his job?

17. What is the probability of getting the individual to retire voluntarily prior to normal retirement age? What amount of time might be required to condition him to this attitude?

18. What are the financial implications of retirement for the individual, considering—

    a. Estimate of financial obligations—housing, children, etc.

    b. His cash income from company—average over last five years,

    c. Estimated other annual income,

    d. Estimated retirement income from company if retired early,

    e. Estimated retirement income from company at normal retirement age,

    f. Ratio of early retirement income to normal retirement income and to present income?

19. What type of financial arrangement would make the man look with favor on early retirement?

II. Retention Beyond Normal Retirement Age

1. Has the question of retention of this individual been raised because of—

    a. Lack of a replacement,

    b. Temporary need for his special skills—if so, for how long,

    c. Fear of losing individual to a competitor,

    d. Executive's need for more income than the pension plan will provide,

    e. Man retains a high level of competence?

2. What is the mental and physical health of the man based on—
   a. Recent history,
   b. Current situation,
   c. Prospective problems?

3. What is the appraisal of his recent job performance, in terms of—
   a. Teamwork
   b. Leadership and organization,
   c. Initiative,
   d. Contribution to profit,
   e. Decisiveness—reaction to crisis,
   f. Technical competence?

4. What is the situation regarding a satisfactory replacement—
   a. Replacement impossible?
   b. Replacement not needed?
   c. Within specified time period?

5. What action toward replacement would be taken if this man were to be totally and permanently incapacitated tomorrow?

6. Does retention of this individual result in deferring the promotion of another man? What will be the result of this?

7. Would deferment of this individual's retirement delay planned organizational changes?

8. What precedent would be established, strengthened, or broken, by retention of this man?

9. Is the nature of the project that the individual is involved in such that his retention is warranted?

10. To what extent may the individual himself, or his immediate superior, have developed and fortified the reasons which give rise to his becoming indispensable at the normal retirement age?

11. What has been past practice in similar cases at comparable job levels in the company?
12. What action, other than retention as a full-time employee, could be taken to still solve the problem connected with the request for retention of this individual?

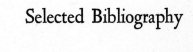

Selected Bibliography

SELECTED BIBLIOGRAPHY

"Adjustment in Retirement," *Journal of Social Issues,* Vol. 14, No. 2, 1958, entire issue.

"Aging and Retirement," *American Journal of Sociology,* January, 1954, entire issue.

Bailey, Earl L., and Thompson, G. Clark, "Company Relations with Retired Executives," *Conference Board Business Record,* June, 1959, pp. 280-284.

Bell Telephone Company of Pennsylvania and The Diamond State Telephone Company, *Survey on Preparation for Retirement,* A Report by the Benefit Office, January, 1956, 12 pp.

Bennett, George K., "A Psychologist's View of Retirement Policies," *Industrial Medicine and Surgery,* Vol. 23, No. 5, May, 1954, pp. 209-212.

Brown, Rollo Walter, "Must 65 Be Fatal?" *The Atlantic Monthly,* December, 1950, pp. 51-54.

Couper, Walter J., and Vaughan, Roger, *Pension Planning, Experience and Trends,* New York: Industrial Relations Counselors, Inc., 1954, (Industrial Relations Monograph, No. 16), 245 pp.

Crook, G. Hamilton, and Heinstein, Martin, *The Older Worker in Industry: A Study of the Attitudes of Industrial Workers Toward Aging and Retirement,* Berkeley: University of California, Institute of Industrial Relations, 1958, 143 pp.

Donahue, Wilma, et al., eds., *Free Time, Challenge to Later Maturity,* Ann Arbor: University of Michigan Press, 1958, 172 pp.

Donahue, Wilma, and Tibbitts, Clark, eds., *The New Frontiers of Aging,* Ann Arbor: University of Michigan Press, 1957, 209 pp.

Dublin, L. I., Lotka, A. J., and Spiegelman, M., *Length of Life, A Study of the Life Table,* rev. ed., New York: The Ronald Press Company, 1949, 379 pp.

Editors of Fortune, *The Executive Life,* Garden City, New York: Doubleday & Company, Inc., 1956, 223 pp.

Friedmann, Eugene, and Havighurst, Robert J., *Meaning of Work and Retirement,* Chicago: University of Chicago Press, 1954, 197 pp.

Hall, Challis A., Jr., *Effects of Taxation: Executive Compensation and Retirement Plans,* Boston: Harvard University—Graduate School of Business, 1951, 365 pp.

Havighurst, Robert J., "Flexibility and the Social Roles of the Retired," *The American Journal of Sociology,* January, 1954, pp. 309-311.

Janney, J. Elliott, "Company Presidents Look at Themselves," *Harvard Business Review,* May-June, 1952, pp. 59-70.

Johnson, George E., "Is a Compulsory Retirement Age Ever Justified?" *Management Review,* November, 1951, pp. 666-667.

Lerner, Max, *America as a Civilization,* New York: Simon and Schuster, 1957, 1,036 pp.

Mason, Edward S., ed., *The Corporation in Modern Society,* Cambridge, Massachusetts: Harvard University Press, 1959, 335 pp.

Mathiasen, Geneva, ed., *Criteria for Retirement,* New York: G. P. Putnam's Sons, 1953, 233 pp.

Mathiasen, Geneva, *Flexible Retirement; Evolving Policies and Programs for Industry and Labor,* New York: G. P. Putnam's Sons, 1957, 226 pp.

Moore, Elon H., *Nature of Retirement,* New York: The Macmillan Company, 1959, 217 pp.

Newcomer, Mabel, *The Big Business Executive,* New York: Columbia University Press, 1955, 164 pp.

Perrow, Charles, "Are Retirement Adjustment Programs Necessary?" *Harvard Business Review*, July-August, 1957, pp. 109-
115.

Pollack, Otto, *Positive Experiences in Retirement*, Philadelphia:
University of Pennsylvania—Wharton School of Finance and
Commerce, Pension Research Council, 1957, 52 pp.

———, *Social Aspects of Retirement*, Philadelphia: University of
Pennsylvania—Wharton School of Finance and Commerce,
Pension Research Council, 1956, 47 pp.

Riesman, David, Glazer, Nathan, and Denney, Reuel, *The Lonely
Crowd*, Garden City, New York: Doubleday & Company,
Inc., 1953, 359 pp.

Sanders, Thomas H., *Effects of Taxation on Executives*, Boston:
Harvard University, Graduate School of Business Administration, 1951, 229 pp.

Sargent, Dwight S., *Some Economic Aspects of Compulsory Retirement at Age 65 Versus a Flexible Policy or a Compulsory
Retirement Age at 68*, Presented at Personnel Conference for
Savings Banks Association, New York, October 17, 1958,
6 pp., and appendix (multilithed).

Sheldon, Henry D., *The Older Population of the United States*,
New York: John Wiley and Sons, 1958, 223 pp.

Shultz, E. B., "Selective Retirement and Preretirement Counseling in the TVA," *Industrial and Labor Relations Review*,
January, 1959, pp. 206-213.

"Social Contributions by the Aging," *The Annals*, January, 1952,
entire issue.

Steiner, Peter O., and Dorfman, Robert, *Economic Status of the
Aged*, Berkeley: University of California Press, 1957, 296 pp.

Stryker, Perrin, "How to Retire Executives," *Fortune*, June, 1952,
pp. 110-111, 174.

Tibbitts, Clark, "Retirement Problems in American Society,"
The American Journal of Sociology, January, 1954, pp. 303-
307.

———, ed., *Handbook of Social Gerontology*, Chicago: University of Chicago Press, 1960, 770 pp.

United States Senate—Committee on Labor and Public Welfare,
Federal Programs for the Aged and Aging, Hearings Before

the Subcommittee on Problems of the Aged and Aging, 86th Congress, 1st Session, Washington: Government Printing Office, 1959, 339 pp.

————, *Studies of the Aged and Aging: Employment,* Washington: Government Printing Office, 1957, 49 pp.

Wald, Robert M., and Doty, Roy A., "The Top Executive—A Firsthand Profile," *Harvard Business Review,* July-August, 1954, pp. 45-54.

Wermel, Michael T., and Beideman, Geraldine M., eds., *Industry's Interest in the Older Worker and the Retired Employee, Proceedings of a Conference,* Pasadena: California Institute of Technology, Industrial Relations Section, May, 1960, (BIRC Publication No. 13), 35 pp.

Index

INDEX